PELICAN BOOKS

POLITICAL IDEAS

David Thomson, M.A., Ph.D. (Cantab.), was born
in 1912. He was a Scholar of Sidney Sussex College, 1931–4, when he took First Class Honours
in both parts of the Historical Tripos. He was a
Research Fellow of Sidney Sussex College (1937–
45), a Fellow from 1945 to 1957, and in 1957 became
Master of the College until his death in 1970. He
was a University Lecturer in History. In 1950, and
again in 1953, he was Visiting Professor of Public
Law and Government at Columbia University in
New York.

His other writings include *World History from
1914 to 1961* (1963), *Democracy in France since
1870* (1964), *England in the Nineteenth Century*
and *England in the Twentieth Century* (*Pelican
History of England,* volumes 8 and 9) and *Europe
Since Napoleon* (Pelican edition 1966). He did a
fair amount of journalism and broadcasting on
modern political affairs. He once said: 'I enjoy
lecturing, teaching, and writing; find a don's life
a very busy but a happy one; and believe the
study of history to be the best liberal education
a student can have in the modern world.'

POLITICAL IDEAS

EDITOR

David Thomson

CONTRIBUTORS

D. E. D. Beales

M. Cranston   J. R. Hale

J. Hampden Jackson

A. C. Macintyre   K. R. Minogue

G. C. Morris   C. W. Parkin

R. S. Peters   W. D. J. Cargill Thompson

P. H. Vigor   J. W. N. Watkins

PENGUIN BOOKS

PENGUIN BOOKS

Published by the Penguin Group
27 Wrights Lane, London w8 5tz, England
Viking Penguin Inc., 40 West 23rd Street, New York, New York 10010, USA
Penguin Books Australia Ltd, Ringwood, Victoria, Australia
Penguin Books Canada Ltd, 2801 John Street, Markham, Ontario, Canada l3r 1b4
Penguin Books (NZ) Ltd, 182–190 Wairau Road, Auckland 10, New Zealand

Penguin Books Ltd, Registered Offices: Harmondsworth, Middlesex, England

First published by C. A. Watts & Co. Ltd 1966
Published in Pelican Books 1969
13 15 17 19 20 18 16 14 12

Copyright © C. A. Watts & Co. Ltd, 1966
All rights reserved

Made and printed in Great Britain
by Richard Clay Ltd, Bungay, Suffolk
Set in Monotype Garamond

CONTENTS

Preface   9

1 Introductory: The Nature of Political Ideas   11
   By DAVID THOMSON

2 Machiavelli and the Self-sufficient State   22
   By J. R. HALE (*Professor of Italian at University College,*
   London)

3 Martin Luther and the 'Two Kingdoms'   34
   By W. D. J. CARGILL THOMPSON

4 Thomas Hobbes and the Philosophy of
     Absolutism   53
   By K. R. MINOGUE (*Senior Lecturer in Politics at the*
   London School of Economics and Political Science)

5 John Locke and Government by Consent   67
   By MAURICE CRANSTON (*Professor of Political Science*
   at the London School of Economics and Political Science)

6 Montesquieu and the Varieties of Political
     Experience   81
   By G. C. MORRIS (*Fellow of King's College in the*
   University of Cambridge)

7 Rousseau and the General Will   95
   By THE EDITOR

8 Tom Paine and the Rights of Man   107
   By J. HAMPDEN JACKSON

9 Burke and the Conservative Tradition   118
   By C. W. PARKIN (*Fellow of Clare College in the*
   University of Cambridge)

CONTENTS

10   Hegel and the Nation-State   130
      By R. S. PETERS (*Professor of the Philosophy of Education
      in the London University Institute of Education*)

11   Mazzini and Revolutionary Nationalism   143
      By D. E. D. BEALES (*Fellow of Sidney Sussex College,
      Professor of Modern History in the University of Cambridge*)

12   John Stuart Mill and the Liberty of the
         Individual   154
      By J. W. N. WATKINS (*Professor of Philosophy at
      the London School of Economics and Political Science*)

13   Marx and Modern Capitalism   168
      By P. H. VIGOR (*Consultant in Soviet Affairs,
      Royal Military Academy, Sandhurst*)

14   Recent Political Thought   180
      By A. C. MACINTYRE (*Henry R. Luce Professor of
      Language, Mind and Culture at Wellesley College,
      Massachusetts*)

15   Conclusion: The Idea of Equality   191
      By THE EDITOR

      Index   203

PREFACE

OF the fifteen contributions to this symposium, nine are based upon a series of broadcasts (also entitled 'Political Ideas') produced by Mr Gilbert Phelps in 1964 for the Third Network of the British Broadcasting Corporation. The editor and the publisher are grateful to the BBC and to Mr Phelps, as well as to the contributors, for their ready agreement that the scripts should be used in this way, and for their co-operation in revising them appropriately. The studies of Luther, Hobbes, Montesquieu and Mazzini, as well as the Introduction and the Conclusion, have been specially written for this book. All the contributors share, it would seem, one basic belief: that to stimulate and nourish intellectual curiosity about political ideas is to engage in a worthwhile educational enterprise. It may be hoped that the harvested fruit of their enterprise will serve this purpose.

Sidney Sussex College, Cambridge   D. T.
August, 1965

I

INTRODUCTORY:
THE NATURE OF POLITICAL IDEAS

DAVID THOMSON

THIS little book introduces the most significant ideas discussed by some of the most eminent European political theorists of the last five hundred years. It is thus circumscribed by at least five self-imposed limitations which determine its character.

Its function is introductory. Each contributor has concentrated, in the brief space available, on the task of presenting a few fundamental ideas, often expressed in the great writer's own words or in a careful translation of them. He will have achieved his aim if the reader becomes interested enough to explore these ideas more fully in the writings mentioned at the end of each chapter.

It is concerned only with the most significant political ideas: with the themes mentioned in the titles of the chapters, and with related ideas that are prominent in the theory being discussed. Many other ideas of interest and arguments of relevance, however, are to be found in the other writings indicated in the brief book-lists.

It embraces only a dozen or so out of a potentially much longer list of creative thinkers. Those included have been selected because their ways of thought and the conclusions they reached in their thinking represent different facets of the evolution of government, and of ideas about society and the State which have mattered in modern history and which still matter today. Other writers, of almost equal importance or interest, have perforce been omitted.

It comprises only European political theorists. They form a coherent, if many-sided, tradition of thought which has prevailed increasingly throughout the world in modern times. Quite other traditions of thought exist outside the western world – in India, China, Africa: but it is the confrontation between these different traditions and modes of thought and the western which may come to seem, in retrospect, the most striking characteristic of twentieth-century politics.

Finally, the book includes only writers who have lived during the last five centuries: thereby excluding some of the greatest of all political philosophers, such as Plato and Aristotle in the ancient world, or St Augustine and St Thomas Aquinas in the medieval world. This necessity of selection is offset by the coherence and continuity of development of western culture since the fifteenth-century Renaissance, which merit attention in their own right: and by the fact that an earlier volume in this same series has dealt admirably with the ancient Greeks.*

Within these bounds the theme of the book falls into four consecutive but overlapping parts. The contributors who discuss Machiavelli, Luther and Hobbes deal ultimately with the creation of political sovereignty: with the ideas entailed in the establishment of separate secular governing authorities within distinct territorial areas, each claiming independence of Empire and Church alike externally, and superiority over all other lordships internally. The kingdoms which took shape during the sixteenth and seventeenth centuries in England, France, Spain, Portugal and parts of north-western Europe, set a pace and a pattern of political organization which were to be widely imitated elsewhere.

The second group of thinkers to be examined – two Englishmen John Locke and Tom Paine, two Frenchmen the Baron de Montesquieu and Jean-Jacques Rousseau – are especially concerned in their political theorizing with the problems of relationships between governments and governed: between the sovereign power established within each separate kingdom, and the citizens whose interests, opinions, wishes or rights it claimed to rest upon or was increasingly expected to protect and represent. From the ideas of such thinkers of the

*The Greeks (ed. H. Lloyd-Jones), The New Thinker's Library (1962).

seventeenth and eighteenth centuries sprang the great liberal and constitutional tradition of politics. This tradition was concerned to humanize the operations of political power by principles of 'the rule of law', of basing government on the consent of the governed (or of influential sections of the community), of systems of checks and balances designed to safeguard the freedom and rights of the individual. It culminated in the western liberal-democratic revolution, which comprised the American Declaration of Independence (1776), the rise of movements for parliamentary and radical reforms in Britain, and the French Revolution (1789). These revolutions, and the wars and other turbulent events to which they gave rise, coincided with the beginnings of a vast transformation in the economy of the western world usually (but inadequately) labelled the 'industrial revolution'.

The third sequence of thinkers to be discussed (the Irishman Burke, the Prussian Hegel and the Italian Mazzini) represent the first great political consequence of the age (1789–1848) which experienced the combined ferments of the democratic and industrial revolutions: an outburst of fervent nationalism, when philosophers, prophets and practitioners of politics alike proclaimed a new, dynamic alliance between government and governed in the form of the Nation-State. The sovereign territorial State, it seemed, had found its human content and identity in the Nation, homogeneous and coherent, self-disciplined and loyal: at the same time the community of the governed, it also seemed, had found its fulfilment and salvation in the State, self-sufficient and powerful, popular and sovereign. The idea of the sovereign Nation-State, claiming self-determination and independence, reached its culmination in the post-war settlement of 1919 and the philosophy of President Woodrow Wilson, though it had won its greatest victories in Europe half a century earlier (1870–71) with the political unification of Italy and Germany, and its theoretical apotheosis in Hegel half a century before that.

Meanwhile, too, rival political theories had come into being to challenge some of the doctrines of nationality. On one hand English, American and French liberalism, voiced here by John Stuart Mill, reasserted the claims of individual personality against the new leviathan of excessive governmental authority and (no less important) of the prospective tyranny of mass opinion demanding conformity and uniformity in an urban, industrial, mechanized society. On the other hand Karl Marx diagnosed capitalist society as created by the 'industrial revolution' and evolved a revolutionary theory equally opposed to the Liberal individualism of Mill and to the nationalistic demands of Mazzini. His ideas bore little fruit until the present century. Then they, or derivatives and adaptations of them, captivated the revolutionary movements which won power in Russia, China and much of eastern Europe. The rival 'ideologies' of the cold war of the 1950s thus had their roots in the political ideas of the previous two centuries: which gives to the concluding three chapters a special contemporary relevance.

To suggest this fourfold chronological division into the theorists of sovereignty, of relationships between government and governed, of the Nation-State, and of liberal-democracy and revolutionary communism, is to imply, however, a greater discontinuity of intellectual debate than in fact existed.

The ideas of Hobbes, Locke and Rousseau belong to one category of political theory, in that all invoked the notion of a 'social contract' as a basis for political authority and for reasons why citizens should obey their governments. Ideas of 'social contract', or common agreement as the foundation of Society and of the State, form a link of continuity between the first phase and the second.

Similarly Edmund Burke in his most famous pamphlet, *Reflections on the Revolution in France*, attacks political ideas identified with Rousseau and Paine, and by dint of his constant emphasis on historical precedent, tradition and continuity, takes his place as a philosopher of conservatism and of nationality. At the same time his inherent Whiggery and devotion to parliamentary constitutional government, and his support for the cause of the American rebels against the policies of George III and Lord North, offer a strand of continuity between Locke and Paine on one hand, Mazzini and

Mill on the other; and, at a deeper philosophical level, his sense of the value of an organic community as the indispensable *milieu* of human freedom gives him affinities with his apparent antagonist Rousseau.

John Stuart Mill, likewise, can be seen as a thinker straddling several divisions. As the direct disciple of Jeremy Bentham (1748–1832) he imbibed much of the rationalism of the eighteenth-century *philosophes* and the radical utilitarianism which, from Bentham, can be traced back to Hobbes and to Locke: but his own liberal nationalism gave him affinities with Mazzini, and his sympathy for the victims of competitive capitalism and industrial exploitation led him to adopt policies which, in his own view, entitled him to be called a socialist.

Some of the wisdom to be gained from studying political ideas in this way – through the arguments embodied in the writings of great political philosophers – is, indeed, learning to distrust neat classification of big men or big ideas into sharply defined categories or hostile camps. Apparent opposites may come, in the often surprisingly devious course of time, to belong more obviously together than does either with its contemporary allies. Calvinists and Jesuits in the sixteenth century alike stood for the ideal of a Church-State which, by the very tenacity and ferocity of their quarrels, they ensured should succumb before the one alternative neither of them wanted, a State-Church. Many have noted that the Communists and Fascists of the twentieth century, though bitter enemies in ideology and in domestic and international politics, shared a common devotion to the ideas of single-party, totalitarian dictatorship. They nursed a common hatred of liberal democracy which made such freakish events as the Hitler-Stalin Pact of 1939 seem not unnatural. The English idealist philosopher T. H. Green (1836–82) theorized from premises the very opposite to J. S. Mill's: but in practical politics their views were almost indistinguishable one from the other.

Attaching glib descriptive labels to great thinkers can mislead more often than it helps. The intellectual dangers of it can

best be avoided by changing the labels frequently and by looking for many different regroupings of them. In addition to
the flexible classifications already suggested for the writers
discussed in this book they might be paired in dialogues
(Machiavelli with Luther, and so on) or regrouped into such
differing categories as the following –

(i) exponents of theories of interests (individual or group),
as compared with exponents of theories of opinion, will and
moral purpose;

(ii) those who depict the State as natural or organic, as
compared with those who depict it as artificial or mechanical;

(iii) those who look back to a 'golden age' in the past,
as compared with those who look forward to one in the
future;

(iv) those who look for political action on the part of
the community as a whole, as compared with those who
emphasize the role of heroes or *élites*.

This done, we can look for more wide-embracing categories
still which throw further cross-beams of light on the big
eternal political issues of human freedom, the grounds of
obligation and the limits of obedience, the basis of law and of
loyalty. The remark of an American professor of politics
points one way –

The theory which defines liberty as freedom from political and
social restraints was propounded by Locke, Tocqueville, and Mill,
and it was given full account by Rousseau, Burke, and Marx and
Engels. The demand for political liberty had a definite meaning in
this historical epoch, and the behaviour of states and citizens can
only be understood by referring to the class structure and the
economic institutions of that time.*

Such quests for underlying affinities or alignments can produce strange bedfellows, as Professor Hacker's list shows. It
raises the still wider question (already begged above in the
assumption that it *is* realistic to speak of one 'coherent, if
many-sided, tradition of thought which has increasingly
prevailed throughout the whole world in modern times'):

*Andrew Hacker, *Political Theory: Philosophy, Ideology, Science* (New
York, Macmillan Company, 1961), p. 10.

how far can we think in terms of one unique body of western ideas and modes of thought, a comprehensive 'western intellectual tradition' comprising both Machiavelli and Rousseau, Paine and Marx?

There lies beneath all the theorizing about man and the State hereafter described a common inheritance of ideas from the classical humanism of ancient Greece and Rome and from medieval Christendom. All men imbued with this common heritage tend to insist that individual personality has an ultimate value which must not be sacrificed to the claims either of society as a whole or of government. Even the seemingly most collectivist thinkers, a Hobbes, a Rousseau or a Marx, urging in some moods absolute claims on behalf of the community, can usually be found, under the skin, to have at heart the ultimate claims of individual personality. Strong infusion of the rationalistic, scientific spirit of intellectual curiosity and experiment has often reinforced this underlying individualism.*

The most glaring exception is racialism, especially in the extreme nihilistic form preached – and to a ghastly extent practised – by the German National-Socialist movement of Adolf Hitler. Racialism appears to be at great variance with the central intellectual tradition, and it would require another book to examine it adequately. It is, unfortunately, far from unimportant, and its relevance to our theme will be considered in the Conclusion.

Finally, it may be asked, what benefits can come from studying in this way the big political ideas of the past? First, we must be clear what not to expect, lest in disappointing ourselves we may lose the interest needed to bring substantial benefits.

We should not go to political philosophers as mentors in the practical art of government. Machiavelli wrote *The Prince* in a *genre* of literature already established, of handbooks of advice for rulers. Its notoriety then and since comes from the contrast

*See the thesis expounded by J. Bronowski and B. Mazlish in *The Western Intellectual Tradition* (1960), though they unfortunately end with Hegel.

between the familiar piety of the *genre* and the brutally cynical advice tendered by Machiavelli. It was as if an author had burlesqued the Coronation Service or the Lord's Prayer. Its real message was the necessity for 'arms and the man' – for a secular ruler to have adequate power and the will to use it adroitly. Statesmen seldom have to apprentice themselves to philosophers to learn their job, and even when they adopt political theories as 'creeds' they rarely owe success to the study of political writings. Frederick the Great read and refuted Machiavelli's *Prince*; but when he practised Machiavellian diplomacy himself it was not because he had studied *The Prince*. The 'theory', indeed, is often invented afterwards, as a rationalization of what was decided on empirical or opportunistic grounds.

Nor is the value of studying political philosophy to be assessed historically, on the assumption that the ideas found therein are somehow representative of the age. Political thought, like any other kind of thought, is fully understood only by relating it to the context of time, place and personality in which it occurred. But the ideas of a great thinker are not necessarily, or even probably, 'representative' of the thought of his time. They are more likely to be heretical and unrepresentative. The interest for us of Montesquieu, Paine or Burke lies not in whatever evidence they may provide of how Frenchmen or Englishmen thought in the eighteenth century, but in the insight they offer into how men think at any time. What concerns us is their eternal, not their temporary, qualities and characteristics. What we learn from Rousseau about the ever-present issues of how to attain individual freedom in a community with whose opinions and actions we may often disagree is infinitely more interesting, important and worth while than anything we may learn from him about what Frenchmen thought in the twilight years of the *ancien régime*. Genius is seldom typical of any collectivity, or the best source of information about that collectivity as a whole.

Nor, again, does the importance of great ideas lie mainly in their influence on great events, though the interplay of ideas and events is one of the more fascinating problems of historical study. 'Influence' is extraordinarily difficult to assess and only too often alleged 'influence', on closer scrutiny, is found to be a myth or a speculation. How far the ideas to be found in the American Declaration of Independence are there because Thomas Jefferson and his colleagues had read John Locke or Tom Paine, and just how much of the thinking of Montesquieu and Rousseau found its way, in fact, into the French Declaration of the Rights of Man and of the Citizen in 1789, remain matters of intricate debate and considerable controversy. The way Lenin adapted and modified the ideas of Karl Marx matters at least as much as the extent to which he adopted and assimilated them.

Yet the great political thinkers *are* worth knowing about. They deserve to be read carefully because they are men of genius who concerned themselves with complex human problems which we cannot escape from in our own lives. We may acquire political wisdom from tuning in to the great debate which has lasted so long and to which so many minds of wonderful intellectual subtlety, distinction and creativeness have made contributions. To ignore this debate, when the world is sadly in need of more wisdom in the management of its affairs, would be like neglecting the ideas of Newton and Einstein when we are trying to grapple with problems of modern physics.

But this wisdom will not be acquired, it may be repeated, in the handy form of clever dodges or politicians' 'tricks of the trade', nor as sage rules of thumb to be followed to ensure success in government, nor even as 'principles' universally valid and applicable by practitioners of politics. The 'principles of politics' can be grasped only by the harder route of learning to appreciate the subtle interconnexions of differing ideas and even of apparently (or genuinely) conflicting ways of approaching politics. The debate is many-sided and at times confusing because the matter under debate is itself diversified and often perplexing. There are no ready-made 'solutions'. Indeed, the only certainty is that the slick, simple notion or the short-circuit answer will prove to be least fruitful intellectually and most frustratingly inadequate in practice.

Few political truths, despite the assertion of the framers of the American Declaration of Independence, are really 'self-evident'. The ends pursued by men in society are many, as are the means by which they may choose to pursue them. In a plural society – where many different men form into many different groups for pursuing many ends by many means – it is inevitable that not all ends will be compatible one with another: as inevitable as it is that some means will prove inadequate for attaining the proposed ends, and that some consequences will be those which none of the protagonists desired. In a variegated society in which aims and interests collide, political activity will occur, political ideas evolve, political philosophy flourish. The consequences of this fact for the nature of political ideas will be examined after recalling the highlights of the great debate itself: that is, in the conclusion, rather than the introduction, to this symposium.

Finally, omission from the book of any direct discussion of political theories about relations between States has been dictated mainly by exigencies of space. The ideas of international law and organization, as of imperialism and trusteeship, have an important place in the western traditions of political thought: but their relevance to the contemporary world is such as would demand an additional volume, rather than an additional chapter, to do them justice.

BOOK-LIST

The nature of political activity and ideas, briefly touched on in this introduction, can be studied more fully in –

CRICK, BERNARD, *In Defence of Politics* (London, 1962: new Penguin Books ed. 1964).

PICKLES, DOROTHY M., *Introduction to Politics* (London, 1951: new edition 1964).

VEREKER, CHARLES, *The Development of Political Theory* (London, 1957).

The approach to these questions by means of the great thinkers is illustrated (and defended) by –

HACKER, ANDREW, *Political Theory: Philosophy, Ideology, Science* (New York, 1961).

Of the three volumes (ed. EDWARD MCCHESNEY SAIT and W. T. JONES) entitled *Masters of Political Thought* (London, 1942–1959), the second volume (ed. W. T. JONES) covers the writers from Machiavelli to Bentham, the third (ed. LANE W. LANCASTER) those from Hegel to John Dewey, by means of incisive comments on lengthy extracts.

2

MACHIAVELLI AND
THE SELF-SUFFICIENT STATE

J. R. HALE

WE have probably all used, or thought of using the word 'Machiavellian' to describe some action on the part of a State, a politician or even a friend. By calling an action Machiavellian we mean that it is selfish, cunning and without any moral justification. Behind a remark like 'what a Machiavellian thing to do' lie some four centuries of popular distrust of unchristian and ruthless statecraft, and behind that lies the career of the man Machiavelli himself, who was born in 1469 and died in 1527.

It is my job to try and get behind the prejudice implied in the word Machiavellian and to see what Machiavelli really thought and said. For Machiavelli himself was not Machiavellian in the popular 'wicked' sense of the term, though he was the first man to write of politics as a public responsibility which could not afford to operate according to the rules that governed private morality. He wrote at a time when the vitality of medieval religion had dwindled. But almost as soon as he had written, religious life was kicked awake again by the Protestant Reformation and by the Catholic Reformation that developed, in part at least, as a reaction to it. By the middle of the sixteenth century in fact, Machiavelli's secular approach to politics was considered scandalous. Within a generation from his death Machiavelli the man was turned into Machiavel the bogy.

To see past the bogy we must imagine the sort of world he lived in. The medieval idea that in theory, at least, Europe was a unity, directed politically by the Holy Roman Emperor and spiritually by the Pope, had broken down. States were becoming more and more aware that their destinies were in their own hands, and that they could be advanced by purely national self-interest. Machiavelli's own country, Italy, was divided into a number of small, independent States. All were proud of their inheritance from the splendours of ancient Rome, all were convinced that in culture and intelligence they were far ahead of the other States of Europe, whom they referred to contemptuously as 'barbarians'. Machiavelli was a Florentine, and of all the Italian States Florence, the mother of Dante and Boccaccio, was the most proud, and Machiavelli was the most vigorously patriotic of Florentines. Unless we remember this we shall not understand his attitude to politics.

In 1513, then, on his farm outside Florence, Machiavelli wrote *The Prince*. This was not the only book he wrote, but because it is short, shocking and brilliantly written, it is the only one most people read. This is one of the reasons why Machiavelli has become one of the most misunderstood of writers on the State. *The Prince* is all black and white; dogmatic, extreme, epigrammatic. It is full of unqualified statements. The qualifications do exist, but they are not in *The Prince* and it is worth remembering for a moment, that in judging Machiavelli by *The Prince* we are judging him in terms of half an inch out of a whole shelf of books.

What sort of life then did he lead? In the first place he was a government employee of some importance, working in the Florentine chancery on matters concerning war and foreign policy. He was frequently sent on diplomatic missions outside Florence, both to other Italian States and to France and to Germany. In this way he met most of the influential statesmen of his day. There was Julius II, for instance, the most impetuous and dynamic of Renaissance popes; there were the Emperor Maximilian of Germany and King Louis XII of France; and the man with whom his name has become inseparably connected, the warlike Cesare Borgia, son of Pope Alexander VI (though, needless to say, a pope was not officially supposed to have a son), and brother of Lucrezia Borgia. The dispatches he sent home from these missions take up several inches on his shelf.

He was also a man of letters, one of the greatest Italy has known. He wrote two plays – one of them, *Mandragola*, is the most famous of all Italian comedies – and he translated another from the Latin of Terence. He wrote a celebrated short story, *Belfagor*. He wrote enough poems to fill a not-so-slim volume. He wrote a *History of Florence* and a book on military affairs, *The Art of War*, which remained one of the most influential treatments of the subject throughout the sixteenth century and which was widely plagiarized and translated. And he wrote a long series of comments on Livy's *History of Rome*, called *Discourses on Livy*, in which he discussed at greater length all the issues dealt with in *The Prince*, and it is in this work that most of the qualifications referred to just now are to be found. *The Prince* without the *Discourses* is like *Hamlet* without the Prince of Denmark.

Machiavelli, then, was a man of wide interests and varied accomplishments. He was a dramatist, an experienced diplomatist and a scholar. His works reflect all these interests: they are written with a dramatist's flair for effect, they are based on a personal knowledge of contemporary political affairs, and they are based, too, on a close knowledge of the history of the ancient world, especially that of republican Rome.

But Machiavelli was, above all, practical. He read history because it could teach. Politically, the Italy of his day, plagued by foreign invaders and incapable of forming alliances against them, was in a state of chronic crisis. In history he thought he had found a key to its salvation. Men were already learning from ancient art, law and medicine; it was time, he thought, that they learned political behaviour from ancient history. This is how he puts it in the introduction to the *Discourses* –

When we consider the general respect for antiquity, and how often – to say nothing of other examples – a great price is paid for some fragments of an antique statue, which we are anxious to possess to ornament our houses with, or to give to artists who strive to imitate them in their own works; and when we see, on the other hand, the wonderful examples which the history of ancient kingdoms and republics presents to us, the prodigies of virtue and of wisdom displayed by the kings, captains, citizens, and legislators who have sacrificed themselves for their country, – when we see these, I say, more admired than imitated, or so much neglected that not the least trace of this ancient virtue remains, we cannot but be at the same time as much surprised as afflicted. The more so as in the differences which arise between citizens, or in the maladies to which they are subjected, we see these same people have recourse to the judgements and the remedies prescribed by the ancients. The civil laws are in fact nothing but decisions given by their jurisconsults, and which, reduced to a system, direct our modern jurists in their decisions. And what is the science of medicine, but the experience of ancient physicians, which their successors have taken for their guide? And yet to found a republic, maintain states, to govern a kingdom, organize an army, conduct a war, dispense justice, and extend empires, you will find neither prince, nor republic, nor captain, nor citizen, who has recourse to the examples of antiquity! This neglect, I am persuaded, is due less to the weakness to which the vices of our education have reduced the world, than to the evils caused by the proud indolence which prevails in most of the Christian states, and to the lack of real knowledge of history, the true sense of which is not known, or the spirit of which they do not comprehend. Thus the majority of those who read it take pleasure only in the variety of the events which history relates, without ever thinking of imitating the noble actions, deeming that not only difficult, but impossible; as though heaven, the sun, the elements, and men had changed the order of their motions and power, and were different from what they were in ancient times.

The Prince itself was written before the *Discourses*. It contains many references to ancient history, but all its main points are based on the circumstances of Machiavelli's own political career. It is based in particular on three experiences; his reaction to a famous military scandal in 1499; his first diplomatic mission to France in 1500; and his meeting in 1502 with Cesare Borgia. It is necessary to say a word about each of them, because without knowing something of the political world Machiavelli lived in, we cannot understand *The Prince*.

In 1499 the Florentines were trying to capture the city of Pisa. They had already been trying, without success, for four years. This war meant a great deal to the Florentines. Pisa not only provided a useful outlet to the sea for Florentine trade, but its possession before it revolted in 1495 was a matter of pride and emotion that went beyond its mere usefulness. An English parallel would be the dogged way in which the Tudors tried to keep possession of the not-very-useful Calais. The Florentines had no troops of their own. They hired professionals, mercenaries, men who fought for cash for whomever would hire them. In 1499 Pisa was besieged by a mercenary army under a well-known commander, Paolo Vitelli – well-known, and expensive. In August his guns battered a great breach in the city walls, his men were storming forward when Vitelli himself appeared in the breach and ordered them to retreat, threatening them with his commander's baton.

The news that the attack had been called off was received in Florence with dismay, incomprehension – and with increasing suspicion. What were Vitelli's motives? It became clear that if the attack had been pressed home the Pisans would have surrendered – they had already appointed ambassadors to sue for peace, though this could not have been known to Vitelli. Why then had he called off the attack? Was it because he had reappraised the situation and made a valid military decision, or was he a traitor, in the pay of the Pisans?

The Florentines decided that he was a traitor; they trapped him before he could get away and executed him. Machiavelli knew all about the Vitelli affair, thanks to his position in the chancery, and he was sure that this was the right decision. Mercenaries were not to be trusted. Fighting not for their own state, or for a cause, they were simply concerned in saving their skins and their capital – that is, their troops: they would sell out their civilian employers whenever they thought it would benefit them. For the rest of his life Machiavelli was possessed by the idea that States must be militarily self-sufficient, they must have armies of their own citizens, who would fight devotedly for their families and their way of life. So a prince's first duty is to be a soldier and create an army. Machiavelli later wrote in *The Prince*, where he refers specifically to the Vitelli affair –

A prince must build on sound foundations; otherwise he is bound to come to grief. The main foundations of every state, new states as well as ancient or composite ones, are good laws and good arms; and because you cannot have good laws without good arms, and where there are good arms, good laws inevitably follow, I shall not discuss laws but give my attention to arms.

Now, I say that the arms on which a prince bases the defence of his state are either his own, or mercenary, or auxiliary, or composite. Mercenaries and auxiliaries are useless and dangerous. If a prince bases the defence of his state on mercenaries he will never achieve stability or security. For mercenaries are disunited, thirsty for power, undisciplined, and disloyal; they are brave among their friends and cowards before the enemy; they have no fear of God, they do not keep faith with their fellow men; they avoid defeat just so long as they avoid battle; in peacetime you are despoiled by them, and in wartime by the enemy. The reason for all this is that there is no loyalty or inducement to keep them on the field apart from the little they are paid, and this is not enough to make them want to die for you. They are only too ready to serve in your army when you are not at war; but when war comes they either desert or disperse. I should have little need to labour this point, because the present ruin of Italy has been caused by nothing else but the reliance placed on mercenary troops for so many years.

In the next year Machiavelli went to France, to the court of Louis XII. Louis was an ally of Florence and had provided her with troops for another assault on Pisa. This too had been a disastrous failure. Machiavelli's mission was to persuade Louis that this had not been the fault of Florence but of the indiscipline of his troops.

It was the first time Machiavelli had been outside Italy. When he reached the French court he got a shock. The French had no respect for the Italians, least of all for the Florentines. They derided this little City-State for having no army, for being governed by merchants who were too stingy to spend enough money on preparations for war, and for having a republican form of government which led to endless debate instead of the taking of brisk decisions. Machiavelli even heard his beloved city dismissed as *Ser Nihilo* – Mr Nothing.

This contempt scalded him, but he learned from it. He learned that in the game of politics, as it was then played, it was not enough to be thrifty and clever and cultured; you had to spend money, be able to use force, and to make quick decisions and act dynamically.

And act *ruthlessly*. This next lesson he learned from Cesare Borgia. Cesare, with the support of the Pope his father, was in 1502 engaged in trying to conquer a group of territories in eastern and central Italy which had once belonged to the papacy. He did this with a shrewd mixture of force and cunning. He beguiled his enemies with promises and then hit them hard in the back. The technique worked and Machiavelli watched it work. He was there when the most famous of all Cesare's manoeuvres was carried out, the famous 'massacre of Senigallia' when Cesare invited four of his least reliable captains to a banquet of apparent reconciliation, arrested them, killed two on the spot and sent the others off to be killed elsewhere. Machiavelli admired this device because it restored Cesare's authority and enabled him to get on with his work of constructing a firmly governed State. It had involved deceit, but so, as Machiavelli pointed out, did the successful political actions of other contemporary rulers; and not only small Italian princes but Ferdinand, king of Spain, and Pope Julius II himself.

By this time, in fact, Machiavelli was convinced that the State needed a morality of its own, the morality of success: success in defending itself, and thus guaranteeing the safety of its people, success in conquest when this was necessary to protect its own interests. Statesmen could not, in other words, afford the luxury of acting by the standards of private morality; the stakes were too high, too many people were involved. A private individual should always tell the truth. But a statesman sometimes had to protect the individuals in his care with a lie. This attitude had, of course, always been accepted in practice, it figures prominently in the diplomatic correspondence of the time, but it had not been written down before in the form of a precept. This is how Machiavelli put it in *The Prince* –

It now remains for us to see how a prince should govern his conduct towards his subjects or his friends. I know that this has often been written about before, and so I hope it will not be thought presumptuous for me to do so, as, especially in discussing this subject, I draw up an original set of rules. But since my intention is to say something that will prove of practical use to the inquirer, I have thought it proper to represent things as they are in real truth, rather than as they are imagined. Many have dreamed up republics and principalities which have never in truth been known to exist; the gulf between how one should live and how one does live is so wide that a man who neglects what is actually done for what should be done learns the way to self-destruction rather than self-preservation. The fact is that a man who wants to act virtuously in every way necessarily comes to grief among so many who are not virtuous. Therefore if a prince wants to maintain his rule he must learn how not to be virtuous, and to make use of this or not according to need ...

Everyone realizes how praiseworthy it is for a prince to honour his word and to be straightforward rather than crafty in his dealings; nonetheless contemporary experience shows that princes who have achieved great things have been those who have given their word lightly, who have known how to trick men with their cunning, and who, in the end, have overcome those abiding by honest principles.

It is noteworthy how much Machiavelli sees politics as a battle – a constant struggle for power. All politics, in his sense, are 'power politics'.

You should understand, therefore, that there are two ways of fighting: by law or by force. The first way is natural to men, and the second to beasts. But as the first way often proves inadequate one must needs have recourse to the second. So a prince must understand how to make a nice use of the beast and the man. The ancient writers taught princes about this by an allegory, when they described how Achilles and many other princes of the ancient world were sent to be brought up by Chiron, the centaur, so that he might train them his way. All the allegory means, in making the teacher half beast and half man, is that a prince must know how to act according to the nature of both, and that he cannot survive otherwise.

So, as a prince is forced to know how to act like a beast, he should learn from the fox and the lion; because the lion is defenceless against traps and a fox is defenceless against wolves. Therefore one must be a fox in order to recognize traps, and a lion to frighten off wolves. Those who simply act like lions are stupid. So it follows that a prudent ruler cannot, and should not, honour his word when it places him at a disadvantage and when the reasons for which he made his promise no longer exist. If all men were good, this precept would not be good; but because men are wretched creatures who would not keep their word to you, you need not keep your word to them.

This opinion has rather an ugly sound and it may seem as though Machiavelli is recommending deceit as something positively desirable in itself. The qualification to this opinion appears elsewhere in his writings, especially in a letter of advice he wrote to a young friend who was going on an embassy to Spain. 'It is important,' he said, 'that you should have the reputation of being honest, otherwise no one will trust you. However, from time to time you will have to lie, and then you must carry it off with ease and authority.' I suspect that the advice given to young diplomats today does not differ very much from this.

In *The Prince* Machiavelli talks in terms of the rule of a state by one man, because he thought that the democratic nature of the Florentine constitution had weakened it. But the advice he gives was valid for republics, too, and the form of constitution he preferred was a republican one. This preference was so strong that it led him into pure idealism. Towards the end of his life he wrote a pamphlet of advice to the heads of the Medici family, Pope Leo X and Cardinal Giulio de' Medici who were then ruling Florence almost, but not quite, as princes: parts of the old republican constitution were still allowed to function. He advised them to revitalize it, so that on their deaths – they were churchmen and could not, or should not, have children – Florence would be able to function as a vigorous republic again. But this was a dream. The idea of monarchy was strengthening all over Europe. There was a younger branch of the Medici ready to jump in on the deaths of Leo and Giulio and this they did, finally extinguishing all traces of Florence's republican past.

Machiavelli, then, if we look at the whole shelf and not just at the half inch of *The Prince*, was not a defender of tyranny, though he advised strong action; he did not revel in deceit, though he thought it sometimes necessary. But he did preach on a text that was found congenial at the time and has had a famous history: the text that the State has autonomous values of its own, and that political behaviour should be determined not by an appeal to Christian morality or private conscience but to *raison d'état* – reason of State. A State was not a fragment of Christendom or of any other supra-national abstraction, it was itself; it should make its own rules. It should make itself as strong as possible so that it would not have to depend on others, on allies. It should avoid neutrality, inactivity, like the plague. Machiavelli harps time after time on the need for active vigilance. He despised citizens who opted out of the responsibilities of government, who preferred to study books or collect paintings rather than serve their country as magistrates or soldiers. He despised those – and there were many of them during the Renaissance – who thought despairingly that men could not help themselves, that they were the playthings of Fortune. Machiavelli agreed that Fortune played a large part in human affairs, but to guard against this sense of helplessness he wrote, towards the end of *The Prince*, a chapter on Fortune where he likens it to a flood which, though powerful, can be dyked and dammed into the service of man, or he says that she is a woman – and can therefore be beaten into submission. His advice is 'don't beat the breast – act!'

I compare fortune to one of those violent rivers which, when they are enraged, flood the plains, tear down trees and buildings, wash soil from one place to deposit it in another. Everyone flees before them, everybody yields to their impetus, there is no possibility of resistance. Yet although such is their nature, it does not follow that when they are flowing quietly one cannot take precautions, constructing dykes and embankments so that when the river is in flood it runs into a canal or else its impetus is less wild and dangerous. So it is with fortune. She shows her power where there is no force to hold her in check; and her impetus is felt where she knows there are no embankments and dykes built to restrain her.

If you consider Italy, the theatre of those changes and variations I mentioned, which first appeared here, you will see that she is a country without embankments and without dykes: for if Italy had been adequately reinforced, like Germany, Spain, and France, either this flood would not have caused the great changes it has, or it would not have swept in at all ...

But, confining myself now to particular circumstances, I say that we see that some princes flourish one day and come to grief the next, without appearing to have changed in character or any other way. This I believe arises, first, for the reasons discussed at length earlier on, that is, that those princes who are utterly dependent on fortune come to grief when their fortune changes. I also believe that the one who adapts his policy to the times prospers, and like-wise that the one whose policy clashes with the demands of the times does not ...

I conclude, therefore, that as fortune is changeable while men are obstinate in their ways, men prosper so long as fortune and policy are in accord, and when there is a clash they fail. I hold strongly to this: that it is better to be impetuous than circumspect; because fortune is a woman and if she is to be submissive it is necessary to beat and coerce her. Experience shows that she is more often sub-dued by men who do this than by those who act coldly.

How far the actions of later statesmen were affected by Machiavelli's writings is almost impossible to say. Those who quoted him most were, I think, those who wanted chapter and verse to quote as justification for their own instincts. And much of what he wrote can be quoted against the grain of his own convictions. Take this passage from the *Discourses*, for example –

When it is a question of saving the Fatherland, one should not stop for a moment to consider whether something is lawful or unlaw-ful, gentle or cruel, laudable or shameful; but putting aside every other consideration, one ought to follow out to the end whatever resolve will save the life of the state and preserve its freedom.

Knowing Machiavelli as a man, a lover of the republican freedom that had made Florence great in the past, we can sense the true significance of this. But it can also be used to justify indiscriminate conquest or the burning of Jews.

Machiavelli's assumption that the State must pursue a

policy of self-interest in terms of *raison d'état*, not of bible morality, was later echoed by theorists like Hegel, and men of action like Bismarck and Hitler. Today the problem which Machiavelli stated is as urgent as ever. In his time European Christian unity had practically vanished as an ideal, and States were making up their own rules of behaviour. In our own day we realize that these rules lead to war, and could lead to universal destruction. We want to go back to the idea of unity and to extend it from European to world unity. This cannot be achieved merely by fear of the bomb. Do we perhaps need a philosophy that echoes Machiavelli's belief that a certain way of life is worth protecting by force, but which contradicts his assumption that every State is justified in fighting for its own version of that way of life? We can throw away Machiavel the bogy, but, if we are to think realistically about politics, the State and the super-State, perhaps we still need the pugnacious common sense of Machiavelli the man.

BOOK-LIST

The best biography is by ROBERTO RIDOLFI, first published in Italian (1954) and translated into English by CECIL GRAYSON, as *The Life of Niccolò Machiavelli* (Routledge, 1963). A shorter work, which attempts to fit the development of Machiavelli's ideas into the historical circumstances of his own day, is J. R. HALE, *Machiavelli and Renaissance Italy* (Teach Yourself History Series, 1961). HERBERT BUTTERFIELD, *The Statecraft of Machiavelli* (1940) is available. J. H. WHITFIELD, *Machiavelli* (1947) is out of print but obtainable in good public libraries. So is the edition of *The Prince* by L. A. BURD (1891) which contains an essay on Machiavelli by Lord Acton. The influence of Machiavelli's ideas is studied in *Machiavellism, the Doctrine of Raison d'État and its Place in Modern History* by the great German historian FRIEDRICH MEINECKE; it was translated by DOUGLAS SCOTT (Routledge, 1957). *The Prince* may be read in an excellent translation by GEORGE BULL, published by Penguin. The passages from *The Prince* quoted are from Mr Bull's translation; those from the *Discourses* are taken from the translation by CHRISTIANE. DETMOLD in the Modern Library edition.

3

MARTIN LUTHER AND THE 'TWO KINGDOMS'

W. D. J. CARGILL THÓMPSON

PROFESSOR R. H. TAWNEY, in a moment of inspired frustration, once compared Luther's utterances on social questions to 'the occasional explosions of a capricious volcano, with only a rare flash of light amid the torrent of smoke and flame', adding gloomily that 'it is idle to scan them for a coherent and consistent doctrine'. More commonly Luther has been accused of being an exponent of the modern doctrine of the 'religion of the State', even of being a precursor of Hitler. Luther himself was convinced that he had made important contributions to political thought. What is the truth of the matter?

That he was not a political thinker in the conventional sense is undeniable. He had no conception such as Machiavelli's of politics as an end in itself and little interest in the actual workings of society. Luther's approach to politics was theological. For him all political problems were ultimately theological problems, aspects of the larger problem of man's relationship with God. Luther may not have been a political philosopher like Hobbes or Rousseau; he was undoubtedly a political theologian. Far from turning his back on the world, he was deeply involved in it. As a pastor he conceived it to be as much part of his duty to instruct his flock on their temporal responsibilities as to prepare them for the spiritual life of the world to come. From the moment that he emerged into the limelight in 1518 until his death in 1546 he dealt with virtually every social problem of the day – usury, mendicancy, prostitution, the care of the poor, the provision of education, as well as with such fundamental issues of principle as the limits of political obedience and the relations of civil and ecclesiastical authority.

Luther was not a systematic theologian: he never attempted to present a comprehensive exposition of his teaching in the manner of Calvin's *Institutes*. To find out what he has to say, one has to comb through an enormous variety of works – tracts, sermons, polemical pamphlets, biblical commentaries – many of them written at great speed in the course of a hectic and astonishingly prolific life. Even his most important political tract, *Of Temporal Government* (1523), was written to meet the needs of a particular crisis provoked by the attempts of some German princes to prohibit the distribution of Luther's New Testament. But underlying all Luther's writings there is a fundamental coherence of thought which stems from the unity of his theological doctrines. His political ideas are derived from a consistent set of principles which have their roots in his fundamental conception of the way in which God governs the universe. This is not to say that Luther was never inconsistent in his political thought. On certain major issues – most notably, the role of the magistrate in the Church and the treatment of heretics – he did undoubtedly shift his ground in the course of his career. But he was not the self-contradictory opportunist that he is sometimes portrayed as being; moreover, when he did alter his position he was usually well aware that he was doing so, and he would go to elaborate lengths to show that he had not really sacrificed his principles.

Luther's boast that he had transformed men's understanding of the State was not unjustified. In terms of late medieval political theory his ideas were revolutionary, for they challenged the theological assumptions which underlay the traditional medieval doctrine of the supremacy of the Church over the State. The claims of the medieval Church to be the ultimate arbiter of temporal affairs rested largely on the sacramental conception of the Church and the priesthood. According to the official teaching of the Church, the clergy occupied a special position between man and God, for it was only through the sacraments of the Church that men could be brought to salvation. They constituted a separate order set apart from the laity by their ordination and endowed with responsibility for the welfare of men's souls and for the oversight of their temporal lives; they were in a sense mediators between God and man, for they alone could perform the miracle of the Mass and offer up the body and blood of Christ as a sacrifice for the sins of mankind, just as they alone possessed the power of the Keys and had the right to remit sins by the sacrament of absolution or to consign men to everlasting damnation.

Luther's theology involved the complete rejection of the sacramental claims of the Church. He taught that men were justified by God's grace alone and that all that was necessary was to have faith in the saving power of His mercy; in place of the Catholic doctrine of the Mass as a propitiatory sacrifice offered up daily by the priest for the sins of his flock, he taught that men were redeemed by Christ's death alone and that it was blasphemous to suggest that any other form of sacrifice was needed; in place of the Church's claim to control the power of the Keys, he held that the forgiveness of sins was dependent on repentance, and not on priestly absolution; while in place of the idea that the clergy constituted a separate order or spiritual estate, distinct from and superior to the laity, he put forward the doctrine of the Priesthood of All Believers – the belief that there was no essential distinction between priests and laymen, since all those who truly believed shared equally in the priesthood of Christ.

At the same time Luther challenged the papal doctrine of the Two Swords, with its claim that the Pope was the ultimate source of all authority, temporal as well as spiritual, by insisting that temporal rulers derived their power directly from God and that the functions of the clergy were purely spiritual, since they were concerned only with the ministry of the Word and the sacraments. Equally revolutionary in the context of late medieval political thought was his insistence on the doctrine of non-resistance, for it attacked the theory which had been gaining ground since the thirteenth century that subjects had a natural right to resist a tyrannical ruler, as well as providing a further argument against the Pope's claim to be able to depose evil rulers at will.

Not all these ideas were new. For centuries it had been a common cry among imperial apologists and ecclesiastical reformers alike that the clergy should confine themselves to their spiritual functions and not attempt to usurp the authority of secular rulers. The doctrine of non-resistance had a respectable ancestry going back to Carolingian times and beyond. What was novel was the impact which these ideas achieved in Luther's hands. The spread of the Reformation led to a general upheaval in political thinking which was the direct consequence of his theology, although the final outcome was sometimes very different from what he had intended.

Luther was, in many ways, an essentially medieval figure. Both by background and outlook he belonged not to the Renaissance but to the world of late-medieval German piety. He was born in 1483 at Eisleben in Thuringia, the son of a Saxon peasant who had left the land for the Thuringian copper-mines and who had succeeded in establishing himself as a small master. Although Luther liked to boast of his peasant origins he was more of a townsman than a peasant; for he grew up in the small town of Mansfeld, to which his parents had moved shortly after his birth and where his father was at one time a town-councillor. He remained something of a German burgher at heart – solidly middle-class in his social attitudes, contemptuous of the peasantry and the lower classes whom he liked to speak of disparagingly as *Herr Omnes*, conservative in his respect for the sanctity of the existing social order, yet always independent and as ready to speak out freely against princes and nobles as against the peasants.

Luther's parents were prosperous enough to be able to afford a bourgeois education for their son, and in 1501 he was sent to the University of Erfurt with the intention of becoming a lawyer. In 1505 the course of his life was changed by an event which he interpreted at the time as a call from God. Returning to Erfurt from a visit to his parents, he was caught in a thunderstorm and narrowly escaped being killed when a flash of lightning struck him to the ground. Convinced that this was a sign from heaven, he vowed to become a monk. A month later he entered the house of the Augustinian Order in Erfurt. Luther's choice was deliberate, for the Augustinians of Erfurt belonged to the reformed branch of the Order, noted for its strict observance of the monastic rule. They were also closely associated with the university and after his year's novitiate Luther was encouraged by his superiors to proceed with his theological studies in preparation for an eventual academic career. In 1508 (having been ordained priest the previous year) he was sent to the new University of Wittenberg, where he lectured in the Arts Faculty on Aristotle. Luther's first visit to Wittenberg was brief; the following year he was recalled to Erfurt, but three years later he returned to Wittenberg as Professor of Biblical Theology. This time the move was to be permanent: Luther was still under thirty but for the rest of his life he remained a university professor at Wittenberg, lecturing day in and day out on the books of the Bible, throughout all the years that he was leading the struggle against Rome.

During the first half-dozen years of his professorship at Wittenberg he arrived at the idea which was to become the foundation of his teaching and the mainspring of the Reformation, the doctrine of Justification by Faith – the belief that human nature is so corrupted by sin that man is incapable of attaining salvation by his own efforts, and can be saved only by God's grace which is freely given to those who believe in Christ, through whom alone they are made just or righteous and their sins are forgiven. Behind the doctrine of Justification by Faith lay Luther's personal struggle to find assurance of salvation: it represented his answer to the problem which had tormented him throughout his years as a monk and which had driven him at times to the edge of despair, the problem of how to reconcile his sense of the absolute righteousness of God with his consciousness of his own utter worthlessness as a creature of sin.

Luther's theology of Justification by Faith involved a complete reorientation in men's approach to religion. It replaced the medieval belief that it was possible for men to acquire merit with God through the performance of good works, aided by the sacraments of the Church, by the idea that salvation was entirely dependent on God's grace and that man could not contribute to it in any way. Yet it is doubtful how far Luther himself recognized the revolutionary consequences of his teaching at the beginning; at most he saw himself as having arrived at a deeper understanding of what the Church had always taught. It was only with the outbreak of the Indulgences controversy in 1517 that the implications of his theology began to emerge, although even then he had no intention of launching a general attack on the Church. It was the opposition of his critics which first drove him to go further than trying to correct a particular abuse.

Between 1518 and 1520 Luther's ideas developed rapidly. From attacking Indulgences he was led on to challenge the Church's claim to be the final arbiter in matters of doctrine and to take his stand on the authority of scripture alone. Other equally revolutionary doctrines followed, most of them implicit in the concept of Justification by Faith – the idea that the true Church was not to be identified with any particular earthly institution, but was the invisible society of the elect, the *communio sanctorum,* who constituted the true Body of Christ; the concepts of Christian Liberty and the Priesthood of All Believers; his new understanding of the relationship of Law and Gospel; and his condemnation of transubstantiation and the Catholic doctrine of the sacraments. By 1520 when he published his three famous 'Reformation Treatises' – the *Address to the Christian Nobility of the German Nation, On Christian Liberty*, and *The Babylonian Captivity of the Church* – the main principles of his theology were established.

Luther's political theory had its origins in his theology of these years. Many of his leading ideas can be found in such writings as the *Sermon on Good Works* and the *Address to the Christian Nobility* of 1520, although it was not until 1523 that he attempted to develop his views into a coherent doctrine of the State in his treatise *Of Temporal Government*. Like his theology, Luther's political theory was firmly grounded on scripture, especially on such texts as Romans xiii and I Peter ii with their emphasis on the divine character of all temporal authority and the duty of Christian obedience. But it was never simply a collection of biblical tags; it was a complex and carefully worked-out system, the logical outgrowth of his theological beliefs about the nature of man's relationships with God.

Underlying Luther's political thought are two concepts which are central to his theology as a whole – the doctrine of the 'Two Kingdoms' or 'Regiments' (*die zwei Reiche* or *zwei Regimente*) through which God governs the world; and the doctrine, which is closely related to it, of the eternal conflict between the Kingdom of God and the Kingdom of the Devil. Luther's doctrine of the Two Kingdoms or Regiments is one of the most important and one of the most complex elements in his theology, for it runs through all his thinking not only about politics and society, and the relations of Church and State, but also about justification and good works, the nature of man and the way in which God operates in the world. At the centre of the doctrine is the idea that God has established two different orders in the world, through which he governs mankind – the spiritual order (*das geistliche Reich* or *Regiment*) through which he brings men to salvation, and the temporal order (*das weltliche Reich* or *Regiment*) through which he provides for man's natural life. These two orders correspond, on the one hand, to the two different facets of God's purpose towards mankind – to the fact that he is at the same time both Creator and Redeemer; and, on the other, to the fact that man stands in two different relationships to God. Man has, as Luther puts it, 'two persons'; he is at once a soul to be saved, a 'spiritual person' who exists only in relation to God, and a 'temporal person' who exists in the world where he is involved in responsibilities towards other people, although here too he is ultimately in relationship with God.

In these two Regiments God operates in very different ways. The spiritual Regiment is essentially an inward government of the soul whose purpose is to lead men to everlasting life. Here God rules through the Holy Spirit and the Word by which he works in men's hearts to turn them from sin and bring them into his eternal kingdom. It is by its nature an invisible government, for although God entrusts the preaching of the Word to human ministers, no man can tell in whose heart the Word operates, since the workings of the Holy Spirit are secret. It is also a purely voluntary rule, a rule of love; for no one can be compelled to believe by force and God wants only those in his kingdom who hear the Word freely and are willing to follow it in the spirit of Christian love.

The character of the temporal Regiment is quite different: it is essentially an external government, a rule of force. It is concerned only with men's outward actions, not with the inward state of their souls; for its purpose is the maintenance of external peace and justice in the world, without which human life would be impossible, and it has nothing to do with the attainment of the eternal righteousness and peace of God's heavenly kingdom, which lie entirely beyond its scope. The symbol of the temporal Regiment is therefore the Sword, which God has entrusted to temporal rulers and magistrates to exercise on his behalf for the punishment of sin and the maintenance of law and order in the world. God, Luther writes –

has erected two forms of government among men. The one spiritual, through the Word and without the sword, through which men may become godly and righteous, so that by such righteousness they may obtain eternal life. And this righteousness he administers through the Word, which he has entrusted to the preachers. The other is a temporal regiment through the sword, so that those who will not become godly and righteous through the Word for eternal life, may nevertheless be compelled through this temporal regiment to become godly and righteous for the purposes of the world. And such righteousness he administers through the sword. And although he will not reward such righteousness with eternal life, he will nonetheless have it so that peace may be maintained among men, and he rewards it with temporal goods. For this reason he gives the temporal government so much wealth, honour and power, which it may rightly enjoy beyond other men, so that it may serve him in administering such temporal righteousness. Therefore God is himself the founder, lord, master, promoter and rewarder of both forms of righteousness, temporal as well as spiritual.

Luther's doctrine of the Two Regiments is closely connected with his second concept, the idea, which he derived from St Augustine, that the human race is divided into two opposing kingdoms, the Kingdom of God and the Kingdom of the World or the Devil –

We must divide Adam's children [he writes] and all mankind into two parts: the first who belong to the Kingdom of God, the rest who belong to the Kingdom of the World. To the Kingdom of God belong all those who are true believers in Christ and who are under Christ. For Christ is the king and lord in the Kingdom of God ... To the Kingdom of the World or under the law belong all those who are not Christian. For few believe and the lesser part live according to the Christian way, which is that ye resist not evil.

On earth these two kingdoms are inextricably mixed together like the wheat and the tares of the parable, for only God knows who really believes and who are the subjects of Satan. But between them there exists a perpetual state of war which will only cease with the end of the world, for Satan is always seeking to overthrow God's kingdom and to extend his dominion over the whole human race.

This conflict is for Luther the dominating factor in the history of mankind. It explains both the nature of human society and the constant presence of war and strife in the world. Because of it God has instituted the two Regiments in their present form: the Word exists for those who belong to God's Kingdom, the temporal sword exists because the majority of men are subjects of the Devil and can only be restrained from evil by force. The two Regiments are in a sense the weapons which God employs in this struggle against the Devil's Kingdom: for through the Word he attempts to draw men's hearts away from Satan and to bring them into willing obedience to himself, while through the sword he punishes those who remain obdurate and who refuse to listen to the teaching of the Word. At the same time the two Regiments stand at the very centre of the conflict; for Satan is always striving to undermine them and to win control of them for himself by tempting the ministers to whom God has entrusted his two Regiments to abuse their authority and to devote themselves to the service of his kingdom instead of to God's.

Luther's theory of the State – or, to be more precise, his theory of government (for like most medieval thinkers he had little conception of the State in its modern abstract sense) – followed naturally from these theological assumptions. Like Augustine, Luther held that government was both a consequence of the sinfulness of human nature and a divine institution. It exists because the vast majority of men are evil. If all men were Christians the sword would be superfluous, since the true Christian is ruled by the Word. It is because the mass of men do not believe in Christ and can only be prevented from sin by force, that God has instituted temporal government, for without it human life would be impossible. 'If it did not exist, no man could survive because of the rest: they would devour one another as the senseless beasts do among themselves.' Luther's view of government has much in common with that of Thomas Hobbes; for, like Hobbes, he sees the State as the only barrier between man and anarchy.

At the same time Luther emphasized the divine character of civil government. Far from assuming that it must be intrinsically evil or corrupt because of its origins, he insisted that it is one of the greatest blessings God has conferred on mankind. It is the means by which God seeks to protect men from the consequences of their own sin and to enable them to live their lives in peace. He speaks of temporal authority in the highest terms – it is 'a wonderful gift of God', 'a great treasure', 'a divine ordinance', while rulers are God's 'agents' and 'ministers' whom God himself refers to in the scriptures as 'gods', since they stand in his place on earth. For Luther princes and magistrates are in a literal sense God's 'instruments'. They may appear to act on their own initiative, but this is only a shadow; it is God who directs all their actions, and they are merely the 'masks' behind which he conceals his power.

This dual conception of government as a divine institution and a barrier against anarchy explains the strength of Luther's attachment to the principle of non-resistance and his horror of rebellion. Since all authority was ordained by God, it followed that rebellion could never be justified under any circumstances, however evil or harsh a ruler might be. Even tyrants derived their power from God and God alone had the right to deprive them of it. 'I will always hold', he declared in a famous passage, 'by that party which suffers rebellion, however unjust its cause, and be opposed to that party which makes rebellion, however just its cause may be, for there can never be rebellion without the spilling of innocent blood and other atrocities.' Rebellion was, in Luther's eyes, the worst of all possible sins, for it threatened the very foundations of civil society. If it was successful, it meant the destruction of government and the triumph of anarchy: even if it failed, it could only be put down at the cost of much bloodshed and disorder –

Rebellion is not just plain murder; but it is like a great fire which sets a land ablaze and lays it waste; therefore rebellion brings with it a land full of murder and bloodshed; it creates widows and orphans and destroys everything, like the greatest of all disasters.

This almost obsessive fear of anarchy inspired Luther's revulsion against the Peasants in 1525 and accounts for, if it does not justify, his hysterical appeal to the princes to suppress the revolt without mercy. For Luther the peasants were guilty of endangering the fabric of law and order, a crime which they made worse by trying to justify their revolt in the name of the Gospel. Although he had sympathized with some of their grievances at the beginning, he had always warned them that he could never countenance rebellion. When rebellion did break out he saw no option but to throw his influence behind the princes.

But if Luther believed that rebellion could never be right he did not teach that princes could do no wrong or that their commands must always be obeyed. Luther's deep-rooted conception of the all-pervading conflict between God and Satan prevented him from having an exaggerated belief in the infallibility of temporal rulers. Princes were particularly exposed by the exalted character of their office to the temptations of Satan, who was constantly seeking to lure them into becoming tyrants, and he repeatedly declared that 'princes were commonly the greatest fools and rogues on earth'. But even so, he pointed out, it was better to have a tyrant than no government at all or a weak ruler; for it was preferable to be able to enjoy half one's possessions in peace than to have them all exposed to the plunder of the world at large. Equally no ruler had an automatic right to obedience: it was the subject's duty to examine all his lord's commands in the light of his own conscience and to refuse to carry them out when they were contrary to divine law or the law of nature, especially when the ruler attempted to lay down what his subjects should believe. In such cases, though the subject had no right to resist his sovereign by force, he must refuse to obey and be prepared, if necessary, to suffer the consequences.

Only on one occasion did Luther seriously modify the principle of non-resistance. In 1531 he allowed himself to be persuaded, under great pressure, that the German princes might have a legal right to take up arms against the Emperor in certain circumstances. Even in this instance he refused to qualify the belief that resistance was contrary to the Gospel, merely insisting that it was a matter for the lawyers to decide whether such a right of resistance was permitted by the constitution of the Empire, in which case there could be no conflict with the teaching of the Gospel, since the Gospel was not concerned with questions which were solely a matter of temporal law.

The doctrine of the Two Regiments also forms the starting-point of Luther's theory of Church and State. The basic principle is the belief that the two Regiments are quite distinct and must on no account be confused. Not only are they entirely independent of one another in the sense that each owes its existence directly to God, but they are also totally different in character. The authority of the clergy is purely spiritual; they are concerned only with the salvation of souls and the ministry of the Word and the Sacraments. Since the rule of the Word rests solely on voluntary obedience, they can have no coercive power of any kind, even in matters of morals, for physical punishment is a matter for the magistrate alone. The most the clergy can do is to exhort sinners to repentance. This does not mean that the ministers of the Word have no right to take any cognizance of the actions of temporal rulers; it is their duty to admonish them if they fall into sin or attempt to abuse their powers, just as it is their duty to instruct all classes on the proper performance of their temporal callings. But their authority is limited to exhortation, and they have no power to threaten rulers with deposition or to incite their subjects to rebellion.

Conversely the authority of temporal rulers is entirely external and coercive. They are precluded from having anything to do with spiritual matters, for the power of the sword extends only over men's lives and actions. It carries no jurisdiction over their souls: 'the temporal Regiment has the law that it can reach no further than over life and goods and what is external on earth. For God cannot and will not allow anyone to rule the soul except himself alone.' The battles of the faith could be fought only with spiritual weapons. He was strongly opposed in theory to any attempt to promote spiritual ends by temporal means, whether it took the form of the employment of force against heretics or the imposition of beliefs by law or the waging of crusades against the Turk in the name of the Gospel. In this Luther's conception of temporal authority differed not only from the traditional medieval view but also from that of the majority of the sixteenth-century reformers. The magistrate, as magistrate, had no responsibilities in spiritual affairs. There was no intrinsic difference between a Christian and a non-Christian ruler except in the spirit in which they exercised their office: both had the same function of enforcing law and order and punishing sin.

At first Luther thought that the chief threat to the principle of the separation of the Regiments was likely to come from the side of the Church. One of his principal charges against the Papacy was that it was guilty of trying to transform the spiritual Regiment into a species of temporal rule, not only by its usurpation of temporal power but also by its efforts to subject men's consciences to the tyranny of Canon Law. Very soon, however, he came to realize that the ecclesiastical ambitions of the princes also constituted a political danger, and some of his most pungent writing was directed against the encroachments of the temporal powers into the sphere of the spiritual Regiment.

Clear as the distinction between the two Regiments might appear in theory, it proved less easy to apply in practice. Almost from the beginning Luther's theory of Church and State ran into difficulties – difficulties which sprang as much from his own inability to carry through his reforms without the support of the temporal authorities, as from the actual ambitions of the princes. One of the most acute problems which confronted the sixteenth-century reformers was how the change-over from Catholicism to Protestantism was to be brought about. The majority of the reformers, including Luther's leading disciple and eventual successor, Philip Melanchthon, resolved it by developing the theory of the *ius reformandi* of the magistrate – the idea that a Christian ruler had an *ex officio* duty to undertake the reform of the Church in his dominions. Luther was prevented from adopting this solution by his doctrine of the distinction between the two Regiments, although in practice he came very near it in his later years, but he never succeeded in developing a viable alternative.

It is sometimes suggested that Luther was totally uninterested in the question of church organization and that he regarded it as a purely external issue which could properly be left to the control of the secular magistrate. Had this been the case, there would have been no problem. Although he came to hold that certain matters, such as the financial organization of the Church and the exercise of the Church's former jurisdiction in probate and matrimonial cases, were external and therefore did belong under the prince, he was never prepared to allow that the prince had any authority beyond that of other Christians in the spiritual government of the Church. In so far as Luther had a clearly defined theory of church government, it was a logical extension of his doctrine of the Priesthood of All Believers. In principle, ultimate authority in spiritual matters belonged to the Church as a whole, the community of true believers, or to the individual congregation. But such a system could operate, if at all, only under settled conditions – when the Church was properly established and there was little dispute about fundamentals (or about who constituted the Church), or alternatively when the congregation was a persecuted minority which had no option but to manage its own affairs. It did not provide an answer to the problem of how the transition from one form of religion to another was to be effected – a problem made more complicated by the fact that Luther was opposed in principle to any attempt to impose reform by compulsion or to deprive the established clergy of their legal rights except by legal means.

At first Luther seems to have believed that reform would come about spontaneously through the inspiration of the Holy Spirit, if only a free General Council of the Church were held. In his *Address to the Christian Nobility* in 1520 he called on the German princes as members of the Priesthood of All Believers to take the initiative in bringing such a Council into existence. These hopes were largely destroyed within twelve months by the Diet of Worms, which revealed how little support Luther could expect from the majority of the princes of the Empire. Even so, he continued for a time to advocate a policy of *laissez faire*, insisting that the accomplishment of reform should not be hastened by force but should be left to the working of the Holy Spirit. But as he became increasingly alarmed by the growth of disorder and the lack of uniformity in the Church, he was driven to accept the need for positive intervention by the temporal authorities.

The turning-point in the development of Luther's views came in 1527 when he joined with several of the other Wittenberg reformers in inviting the Elector of Saxony to initiate a general Visitation of the Church in his territories. Even so he remained acutely aware of the principle of the Two Regiments, and in the Preface which he wrote for the Saxon Visitation Instructions he attempted to show that there had been no fundamental change in his position. In calling on the

Elector to act, he explained, he and his colleagues had been conscious of the absence of any clearly defined authority in the Church. They had appealed to the Elector to take the lead not in his capacity as prince, but solely 'out of Christian love (for as temporal magistrate he has no such obligations) and for the sake of God, to the benefit of the Gospel and the advantage and salvation of the miserable Christians in his Grace's dominions.' At the same time he emphasized that the Injunctions issued by the Visitors should not be regarded as binding commands, but as tokens of faith, to which all godly pastors should submit 'voluntarily and without compulsion, according to the way of love'. However, he deprived this statement of much of its value by adding that, although the prince had no right to use force in spiritual matters, he was obliged by his office to protect his subjects from discord and it would therefore be his duty to banish from his territories anyone who refused to submit. Technically Luther had managed to preserve the distinction between the Regiments. He continued to hold that the magistrate had no *ex officio* authority in the Church and that he could act only in his capacity as an individual Christian. But the distinction was tenuous, and he had in fact opened the way to the eventual domination of the Church by the State which was to become an almost universal feature of Lutheranism.

The same tendency to compromise the spirit, if not the letter, of the doctrine of the Two Regiments can be seen in the history of Luther's attitude to religious toleration. In principle he was committed to the belief that consciences should never be coerced, and at first he was a passionate champion of religious freedom, opposing all suggestions that Catholicism should be put down by force. To the end of his life he maintained that the magistrate had no right to interfere with men's private beliefs. In practice, however, he gradually shifted his ground. As the years went on his views became increasingly illiberal. As early as 1525 he ceased to argue that the Mass should be tolerated and began to insist that the magistrate had a duty to suppress it as an act of blasphemy against God, on the grounds that this did not involve any infringement of men's private beliefs. Later he extended this principle to justify the persecution of Anabaptists and other extremist sects. He argued that anyone who publicly taught doctrines which were contrary to the fundamental articles of Christian faith was guilty of blasphemy and should therefore be silenced, although he still continued to pay lip-service to the view that no one should be punished simply for what he believed. Luther also developed the argument, which he had used in his Preface to the Visitation Instructions of 1527, that the magistrate had the right to enforce religious uniformity on purely secular grounds, since he had a duty to prevent divisions arising among his subjects – an argument which contained the germ of the later doctrine of *cuius regio, eius religio*.

In the long run, perhaps, Luther's most significant contribution to Christian social teaching lay in his concept of man's two callings (itself an integral element in his doctrine of the Two Regiments); for it led to a new emphasis on the importance of man's social responsibilities in the world and on the value of temporal life in general. Although Luther taught that man was saved by Faith alone, he did not teach that the Christian was exempt from the necessity of doing good works and was only concerned with his personal salvation. On the contrary, he insisted that so long as he remained in this life the Christian was bound to engage in the affairs of the world; for besides his spiritual calling to salvation, God has imposed on him a temporal calling in the world in which it is his duty to serve his neighbour, not from the selfish motive of acquiring merit with God, but purely out of the spirit of Christian love. In consequence, the medieval conception of a spiritual hierarchy of callings, some intrinsically holier than others, was false, for by making the attainment of merit the ultimate object of man's earthly activities it distorted the whole ethical basis of human behaviour. The only genuine good works, Luther insisted, were those which were done spontaneously through Christian love and there was therefore no intrinsic difference between one form of temporal calling and another. It was just as possible for a Christian to serve God as a man-servant or a labourer as in the office of a prince or the ministry of the Word. What was important was that he should devote himself whole-heartedly to the duties of his temporal calling in the knowledge that it was a divine institution which God had created for the benefit of mankind.

· Luther's influence as a political thinker is too diverse to be easily assessed. To a large extent his ideas provided the basis of Protestant political theory in the sixteenth century. His belief in the divine character of government and the sinfulness of rebellion was shared by all the early reformers, including Calvin, and it was only in the second half of the sixteenth century that the principle of non-resistance began to be questioned by Knox and Buchanan in Scotland and by Huguenot writers in France. In England passive obedience remained the official creed of the Anglican Church until 1689. Luther did not teach the doctrine of the Divine Right of Kings: his theory that government was divine applied to all forms of political authority, not merely to monarchy, but it can be argued that he contributed to its development. What cannot be maintained is that he encouraged the worship of the State as an end in itself, in the Hegelian or Nazi sense: had he been able to envisage such a concept, he would have regarded it as the grossest form of blasphemy, the antithesis of everything that he had taught.

Luther's impact on the development of the Protestant theory of Church and State was less clear cut, in spite of the fact that all the reformers took his ideas as their starting-point. Each of the leading Protestant churches tended to develop its own solution to the problem, and there were substantial differences of emphasis between Lutherans and Zwinglians, Calvinists and Anglicans. Even within Lutheranism itself Luther's influence was less decisive than might be supposed. The territorial system of church-government, which eventually emerged in most Lutheran States, was contrary to his fundamental doctrine of the distinction between the two Regiments, although he undoubtedly helped to bring it into existence by his reliance on the support of the princes. In theory Luther was strongly opposed to any form of State control over the Church and it was his successors, rather than

Luther himself, who were responsible for giving Lutheranism its notoriously Erastian character.

Luther failed to realize many of his ideas in practice but he attempted to tackle some of the basic problems of political theory, and it is a measure of his lasting importance that in modern Lutheran theology the doctrine of the Two Regiments is still regarded as the essential basis for the construction of a Christian theory of society.

BOOK-LIST

LUTHER, MARTIN, *Selections from his Writings* (ed. by J. Dillenberger, 1961).

LUTHER, MARTIN, *Works* (American Edition, St Louis and Philadelphia, 1955, still in progress), Vol. 45, *The Christian in Society*.

ALLEN, J. W., *A History of Political Thought in the Sixteenth Century* (London, 1928).

BAINTON, ROLAND H., *Here I Stand – a Life of Martin Luther* (New York, 1950).

KRAMM, H. H., *The Theology of Martin Luther* (London, 1947).

RITTER, GERHARD, *Luther – His Life and Work* (translated by John Riches, London, 1963).

RUPP, E. GORDON, *The Righteousness of God* (London, 1951), especially Chapter 13.

4

THOMAS HOBBES AND THE PHILOSOPHY OF ABSOLUTISM

K. R. MINOGUE

THOMAS HOBBES, who was born in the year of the Spanish Armada, 1588, belonged to a generation of thinkers torn between doubt and dogmatism. No set of beliefs was safe from overthrow, and in all fields men felt driven to make radical changes in the knowledge they inherited. This intellectual world supplied numerous models with whose help an enterprising philosopher might bring fresh understanding to the perennial problems of politics. Hobbes chose geometry. Aubrey, the great gossip of the seventeenth century, supplies us here with an appropriate bit of the Hobbes legend. 'He was 40 yeares old,' Aubrey wrote, 'before he looked on Geometry; which happened accidentally. Being in a Gentleman's Library, Euclid's Elements lay open, and 'twas the 47 *El. libri l.* He read the Proposition. *By G –*, sayd he (he would now and then sweare an emphaticall Oath by way of emphasis) *this is impossible!* So he reads the Demonstration of it, which referred him back to such a Proposition; which proposition he read. That referred him to another, which he also read ... This made him in love with Geometry.'

It was not merely the elegance of geometry that caused the love affair. It was also his delight in the fact that if we start off with very simple propositions, and deduce rigorously from them, we shall come to make new and unsuspected discoveries. Perhaps above all Hobbes loved geometry because it was a superb instrument of aggression. He was the kind of controversialist who liked to bludgeon his opponents into complete submission, and geometry seemed the best available means of closing loopholes and silencing quibbles.

53

Hobbes wrote out his political philosophy a number of times in different versions. These culminated in the *Leviathan* which is by common consent his masterpiece. *Leviathan* was published in 1651, at the end of a decade which had, in England, seen a protracted civil war and the decapitation of Charles I. Its date of publication has led many interpreters to suggest that the absolutism of Hobbes's philosophy is a natural consequence of such turbulent events. This unlikely suggestion may be ruled out of court by the fact that his position was substantially worked out before the Civil War began; and before 1642, whilst the continent had been the scene of incessant civil disturbance, England had been enjoying internal peace for one hundred and fifty years. There is no need to seek explanations of Hobbes's opinions in contemporary events, for he explores a vision of mankind as old as Thrasymachus and Epicurus, and as modern as Sigmund Freud.

The *Leviathan*, if it were to leave no loopholes, had to begin not with political realities but with Reality. Hobbes believed that Reality consisted in the motions of bodies. The flight of a bird across the sky and the darting of a thought into a man's mind might both be explained in these fundamental terms. Hobbes is a consistent materialist, who conceived even of God as being a particularly subtle body – an opinion which instantly laid him open to the charge of atheism. He conceived of human beings as highly complicated machines, whose minds collect and manipulate the information fed into them by the five senses. As a mechanist, Hobbes could only describe his men-machines with the help of imagery drawn from the comparatively crude machines of the seventeenth century. 'For what is the *heart*, but a *spring*; and the *nerves*, but so many *strings*; and the *joints*, but so many *wheels*, giving motion to the whole body, such as was intended by the artificer?' In this particular at least, we may improve upon him, for we have available to us the far more sophisticated machinery of the computer age.

Hobbes believed that men are governed in their movements by passions, which are internal motions. These passions have available a particularly useful servant called reason, whose operations, distinguishing men from other animals, lead to the construction of language, argument and science. In a few short chapters, he ranged over most of the traditional problems of philosophy, reinterpreting both philosophy and human psychology in the terms of his simple and (he believed) irrefutable model. He described man as a creature locked up inside his own frame, unable to penetrate the purposes of other men, and well aware that the language which helps to communicate can also be used to deceive. Man grows to knowledge of himself by comparing himself with others, and one passion in particular never ceases to delight him: the feeling of superiority over other men, especially when these other men can be persuaded to recognize it. In modern terms, Hobbes believes that human life is competitive, and seldom entirely free of the fight for symbols of status. Now if we imagine what would happen to a collection of such individual men outside the boundaries of any settled and civilized state, then our picture will resemble what Hobbes considers to be the 'State of nature'.

A state of nature is one of the indispensable theatrical properties of seventeenth-century political thinking. Sometimes it was thought of as the way men were before the growth of governments; at other times it was merely a rational fiction which allowed us to understand the realities of the human condition. Either way, it was a myth made plausible by the reports of travellers returning from the wild non-European parts of the seventeenth-century world, and by European experience in setting up colonial settlements, especially in America. In principle, it provided a solution to contemporary quarrels; but, inevitably, it turned into another arena in which old quarrels were fought out. It was most favoured by those philosophers keen to convince men that governments were limited by the terms of an original contract. One of Hobbes's claims to originality is the way in which he turned a liberal prop into a device for the justification of an absolutist form of government.

There is a famous difficulty which besets any philosopher

who ventures to use the state of nature. If it is a pleasant condition, then the difficulty lies in explaining why men ever abandoned it for the rigours of the scaffold and the tax collector. If on the other hand, it is unpleasant, then the difficulty is to discover *how* men could ever have come together peaceably long enough to make an agreement to escape from it. Now Hobbes's state of nature is perhaps the most famous political nightmare in the history of philosophy. His most telling prose is marshalled to describe its spiritual and material poverty, the chronic fear and insecurity of the lives men lead –

no arts; no letters; no society; and which is worst of all, continual fear, and danger of violent death; and the life of man, solitary, poor, nasty, brutish, and short.

Now it has been often argued that there are always some men whose natural ascendancy over others will lead them to establish a political order. This would be a natural solution to humanity's political problem, and nothing is more consistent in Hobbes than his rejection of any natural solution to political problems. In the patriarchal society of Europe, for example, few beliefs would seem more natural than that, as between men and women, the right of rule lies with the men. But even here Hobbes resists the virtually unanimous belief of his contemporaries.

And whereas some have attributed the dominion to the man only, as being of the more excellent sex; they misreckon in it. For there is not always that difference of strength, or prudence between the man and the woman, as that the right can be determined without war.

All of Hobbes's mocking and ironic personality appears in those last two words: 'without war'. Even the almost universal European convention of patriarchalism remains nothing more than a convention. Hobbes refuses to elevate it to a normative fact of nature. It is never the brute facts, but individual choice, which is decisive.

How then does Hobbes deal with the belief of the natural *élitist*, the opponent who believes that some men, by virtue of blood, ability, or God's election, are naturally endowed with the right to rule? He deals with it by asserting that men are by nature equal. This assertion superficially resembles the kind of political rhetoric with which we are very familiar: the writings of Locke, Paine, Rousseau, and innumerable declarations of rights, all contain assertions that all men are equal. But here as ever we must be on our guard against reducing Hobbes to the commonplaces of other men. He does not believe that equality is one further attribute of the species man. The main fact upon which he bases this assertion is simply that even the stupidest and feeblest of men can, given the right circumstances, dispossess and kill the strongest. Hobbes does not deny any of the manifest inequalities; he merely observes that no human inequality issues in a superiority which is beyond the destructive range of other men. Besides, to deny equality is quarrelsome bad manners –

if nature have made men unequal; yet because men that think themselves equal, will not enter into conditions of peace, but upon equal terms, such equality must be admitted.

There can therefore be no natural growth of government in Hobbes's state of nature. And without government, men are in a desperate condition. Why is this so? One reason is that goods are scarce. 'And therefore if any two men desire the same thing, which nevertheless they cannot both enjoy, they become enemies' and 'endeavour to destroy, or subdue one another.' On the point of scarcity, many philosophers would agree with Hobbes, though they would play down the enmity between men by some such suggestion as that the first possessor of a good has a right to enjoy it, and a right to bequeath it which other men, rationally obedient to the law of nature, will respect. This would be a 'natural' solution to the problem, and Hobbes, quite realistically, will have nothing to do with it.

But even without scarcity in the state of nature men would necessarily distrust one another. I cannot with certainty tell what is going on in the head of another, and my own thoughts tell me that men are deceitful. Other men will threaten me, and I am a threat to them. The difficulty is not that men lack reason: it is rather the fact of being rational and anticipating danger which makes each man the potential enemy of every other man. In other words, if in doubt about the other man's intentions, strike first. But then, it is also rational for other men to strike at me first, for (by the postulate of equality) no matter how weak I am, I may still constitute a threat to them in the future.

Such rational difficulties are compounded by a third: the fact that men are –

continually in competition for honour and dignity ... and consequently amongst men there ariseth on that ground, envy and hatred, and finally war.

Hobbes continually stresses the sheer restlessness of men, the fact that they are never long satisfied with what they have, and 'can relish nothing but what is eminent'. He believes that for many purposes, life may be compared to a race which 'we must suppose to have no other *goal*, nor other *garland*, but being foremost, and in it'. In this race there is no finish and no rest; to put it in the terms which emphasize that Hobbes was rejecting the dominant philosophical tradition of his time, there is no *summum bonum* or highest good. There is, however, a highest evil, and that is 'to forsake the course', or to die. The fear of this most decisive evil is the lever by which man civilizes himself.

This account of human nature has seemed to many of his readers a libel on mankind, and each generation has produced its commentators crying 'not guilty!' Yet in most respects, it is only the sheer force of Hobbes's rhetoric which marks off his view of mankind from that of St Augustine. Hobbes, like Machiavelli, is preoccupied with a problem of behaviour: and both face up to the moral dilemmas of a world in which a just and innocent man may be destroyed unless he acts ruthlessly to preserve himself. Both are diagnosticians saddled with the moral opprobrium of the disease they have studied. Hobbes knew that many of his readers would bridle at his picture of the state of nature, and as we observed at the beginning he was determined to allow no escape from his chain of argument –

It may seem strange [he wrote] to some man, that has not well weighed these things; that nature should thus dissociate, and render men apt to invade, and destroy one another: and he may therefore, not trusting to this inference, made from the passions, desire perhaps to have the same confirmed by experience.

And he goes on to point out that even when we do have government and 'public officers, armed, to revenge all injuries shall be done him', yet each man still locks his chest, bolts his door, and only rides abroad when armed. 'Does he not there as much accuse mankind by his actions, as I do by my words?' Yet, Hobbes continues, the aggressive acts of natural men are natural acts, and cannot sensibly be judged sinful – until the time when they know a law which forbids such acts. And here we have another instance of his rejection of natural solutions: moral judgements are, in his view, nothing else but the variable approvals and disapprovals of men. It is only with the establishment of a sovereign authority that we can arrive at an objective rule of right and wrong.

The state of nature, as a condition of war, is not a semi-historical myth lodged in the distant past; it is an ever-present abyss which we skirt daily, and thankfully but unwisely forget. In well-governed States, we live so happily with the solution that we forget that it *is* a solution, and what it is a solution to. But then there may come a riot, an interregnum between competing armies, a string of mutinies and foreign confusions such as happened in the Congo, or simply a rather severe industrial or racial crisis. The closest that civilized men come to a state of nature is when, as happened in Hobbes's lifetime, a protracted period of peace leads turbulent subjects to challenge the civil power, and the result is a civil war. Then we realize that the peace we have so long innocently enjoyed was a fragile thing. Civil society is not an outgrowth of our nature, as Aristotle argued, but a precarious construction depending on a correct disposition of human wills. How does it come about?

In moments of fear, man may forsake his pride and by reasoning discover the value of peace and the means whereby it may be secured. This knowledge is, for the philosophically inclined, summed up in the nineteen laws of nature Hobbes outlined in Chapters XIV and XV of the *Leviathan*. The fundamental law of nature is that a man should endeavour to bring about peace whenever there is any chance of it; and when there is no chance (as in the state of nature) then nothing morally prevents a man from taking all necessary steps (of which each man is the only possible judge) to protect himself.

The second law of nature shows a way in which peace might be secured; when each man lays down his right of self-protection, and is 'contented with so much liberty against other men, as he would allow other men against himself'. This sounds like an obvious and equitable solution; but we must not forget – Hobbes certainly does not – that such trustful behaviour is hopelessly irrational in the state of nature. For, he remarks several times, 'covenants, without the sword, are but words, and of no strength to secure a man at all'. Therefore the right of self-protection in the state of nature must be transferred to a third party, who becomes the sovereign power and bears in himself (or in themselves, for this sovereign may logically be an assembly of men) the real personality of the State. Thereafter, each act of an adequately powerful sovereign is acknowledged also to be the act of each one of his subjects; and the subjects are said to be *obliged* to obey the sovereign power. Each subject is, like Gulliver, bound by the Lilliputian cords of obligation; should he break them, the sovereign will punish him. Should he escape punishment, however, he will have weakened the State and brought human life that much closer to the state of nature, which is beneficial to no man.

This is an enormous change in human fortunes, and Hobbes argues it closely, binding the reader to exact definitions of such key terms as covenant, covenant of mutual trust, right, liberty, person, transference. Once the stroke has been accomplished, then civilization, art, science, morality, law, peace and tranquillity are able to develop. Indeed, it is not too much to say that only now do human beings come into existence; for part of our understanding of a person must be the fact that he is predictable and it is his responsibilities or obligations which make a man predictable. Even human identity appears in Hobbes not as something natural, but as the difficult outcome of human choices.

From this point on, the *Leviathan* once again reverts to its first character as a deductive system, and abandons the semi-historical narrative which gives such force to the myth of the state of nature. Hobbes now turns to describe the powers of the sovereign, and to defend his account against those many critics, then and now, who feel that all liberty would be crushed by so monstrous a power. What rights does a subject have against the sovereign? The answer is none. Each act that the sovereign performs is, by virtue of the transference of right, *my* act; and even should the sovereign condemn and execute me, there is an important sense in which I am the author of my own execution. This paradox is a logical implication of the fact that I have originally covenanted to authorize *all* acts of the sovereign. This consequence of Hobbesian logic has led most readers to the conclusion that Hobbes is advocating the kind of unrestrained despotism which no modern man would willingly tolerate. And this impression is reinforced when we find that Hobbes denies as illusory any distinction between a monarchy and a tyranny. A tyranny, Hobbes argues, is merely 'monarchy misliked'. Yet the liberal tradition in the West has always made a fundamental distinction between a king and a tyrant.

There is little doubt that Hobbes rather enjoyed shocking people; certainly he makes little attempt to play down certain formally unpalatable features of his argument. But on the power of the sovereign he saw no possibility of evasion. For if we endeavour to balance powers in our constitution, we merely sow the seeds of civil war when the powers fall out. Only a unified and single power can compress an anarchy of wills into the real unity of a State. On the other hand, if we would set up safeguards, then we must create a power that is stronger than the sovereign (for a weaker power would be no safeguard). We then have a super-sovereign, and we could only be protected against *that* by a super-duper sovereign. And so on. Logically it seemed to Hobbes that any adequate picture of a State must include one concentrated power of last resort.

The position is not perhaps as grim as we might imagine. For men have created the Leviathan in order that they may enjoy a secured peace. Without this peace, they are back once more in the state of nature, as is the case with criminals and traitors, for whom the sovereign is an enemy. In these circumstances we have the odd position that the sovereign has a perfect right to attempt to punish the wrongdoer, whilst the latter has an equal right to seek to escape the punishment. This oddity reveals that Hobbes is using the term 'right' in an unusual sense. It is (like the case of 'equality' discussed earlier) one more signal to the attentive reader that, although Hobbes uses, for the most part, the conventional philosophical vocabulary of his time, his meaning is often different and usually a great deal more interesting.

Men renounce their rights only in order to secure peace. It follows that there are some rights which they cannot rationally renounce. They gain nothing by renouncing the right to defend themselves if attacked; nor can they validly covenant to bear witness against themselves, nor to injure themselves. The sovereign cannot validly oblige us to behave in these ways. There is, on the other hand, little that he cannot regulate should he have a mind for it. In his hands lies the disposition of titles and honours. The customs of the country, along with its manners and its common law, continue in force only so long as he permits. All regulation of property and inheritance is in his hands. This case is particularly interesting since it contrasts so strongly with Locke's attempt to entrench property rights in the state of nature, in such a way as to be beyond the meddling of governments. All these powers further exemplify the point we emphasized earlier: that Hobbes resists any pretence at discovering political solutions in nature. Everything is subsumed under the decision of the sovereign. We even find that the sovereign has power to decree what books should be published and what should be taught in the universities. Hobbes was dissatisfied with the teachings of Oxford and Cambridge. He believed that much

reading in the classics inclined young minds to sedition, and
thought that his own book would be a much sounder ground-
ing in the fundamentals of political duty.

This modest suggestion did not commend itself to Hobbes's
contemporaries. The University of Oxford not only failed to
adopt *Leviathan* as a textbook, but burnt it publicly as being
'false, seditious, and impious'. The objection was largely to
his unusual theological opinions. Parliament in 1666 went so
far as to cite the atheism of Hobbes as being among the causes
of the Great Fire of London. It is certainly true that his
materialism led to highly unorthodox positions on such subjects
as God, the soul, and damnation. Whilst claiming to accept the
Christian revelation he considered all descriptions of God to
be metaphorical. By the use of our own intelligence we must
be led to believe of God 'that he is', but we lack the equipment to comprehend 'what he is'. When we use descriptive
terms about God, we succeed only in honouring him, not in
understanding him. This sceptical line of argument cut
directly at the pretensions of many a sectarian of the century.
Hobbes's attitude to miracles foreshadows that of Hume and
Voltaire in the next century –

For such is the ignorance and aptitude to error generally of all
men, but especially of them that have not much knowledge of
natural causes, and of the nature and interests of men; as by innumerable and easy tricks to be abused.

When we hear of miracles, the real issue is 'in plain terms,
whether the report be true, or a lie'. Each man must make up
his own mind. But men's judgements may differ, and on
emotional questions of this kind, their differences of reasoning
may lead to civil disturbance. When it comes to action, Hobbes
tells us in a phrase that summarizes his attitude on nearly all
such questions 'the private reason must submit to the public;
that is to say, to God's lieutenant'.

This willingness to submit did not please the clergy; nor did
it please the English Tories whose view of the duties of the
citizen might superficially seem to resemble those of Hobbes
himself. The crucial disagreement concerns the source of

political authority. The Tories, following the doctrine of monarchy by divine right, believed that royal authority was a mystery stemming directly from God's will. Hobbes, by contrast, had been led both by his temperament and his method, to attain a superficially similar result from very different premisses. The authority of the Hobbesian sovereign comes from the authorization of his subjects; it comes, that is, from the consent of the individuals who make up the State. The consent is given under conditions so fearful as to allow of no alternative; and it is a blanket consent which the subjects cannot modify to suit their convenience. But it is, all the same, popular consent; and even so remote an admission of the democratic principle may have seemed to the emotional Tories of the later Stuart period to be a beginning to all manner of unpalatable consequences. This irony – that Hobbes the absolutist should be detested for the traces of democracy in his system – has been expanded by some historians of thought into an interpretation of Hobbes as the source of the revolutionary doctrine of the rights of man.

Hobbes has had a bad press in the last three centuries, yet in our generation he is appreciated as he has seldom been before. Any sensitive reader of Hobbes will be able to work out why this is so. For to read the *Leviathan* is to experience a sensation of nakedness. In the state of nature we find ourselves stripped of all security and confronted by the hostility of all other men. And even when we find ourselves subjects of a sovereign, the little shelter we have now acquired against the random invasions of our fellows does not let us forget that nothing guarantees us against the invasions of the sovereign himself. Modern liberal political theory has tried to protect us against this form of nakedness by the fig-leaf of guarantees: by declarations of natural rights, or checks and balances, or faith in the sovereignty of the people. The argument of the *Leviathan* is that no guarantees are or ever could be securities against oppression; and that some guarantees (such as independent parliaments) are an open invitation to civil war. In the generations that followed Hobbes, the main preoccupation of the most articulate members of the political community was to impose constitutional limitations upon the actions of governments. The worst political sin was thought to be arbitrary government action, and the main legacy of that period has been the attitude summed up in Lord Acton's remark: 'Power tends to corrupt, and absolute power corrupts absolutely.'

Our attitude to Hobbes, then, is partly determined by our judgement of where political danger lies. If we see governments as the main threat, and consequently take little notice of the behaviour of peoples, then we will find that Hobbes rubs our noses in facts we would much rather forget. But the twentieth century has provided us with so many cases of nasty popular turbulence that we are much more disposed to look twice at a philosophy that does not pretend that there are guarantees of justice to be found in politics. We too, like Hobbes, have made the discovery that the business of politics is peace, and that those who believe that politics is for enforcing truth will achieve neither truth nor peace. There is a familiar way of making this point: we are sympathetic to Hobbes because we too live in an age of doubt.

This new sympathy has led us to recognize that the *Leviathan* is an endlessly fascinating and subtle achievement of reasoning. And in the process, we have discovered something else. Fifty years ago C. E. Vaughan argued that the *Leviathan* breathed a passionate hatred of individuality. The principle behind this judgement is that individualism flowers under a weak and limited government, and that the purpose of a strong government is to keep individuals in check. Yet it is on the contrary clear to us that the main and perhaps unique distinction of Hobbes's political philosophy is that it never for a moment loses sight of man as a rational individualist. Men at most times are not individualists because they submerge themselves in roles. Only at unpredictable intervals do they emerge from their roles and confront each other as naked wills. It is just this kind of confrontation which Hobbes made the touchstone of political organization. If men are frequently to emerge, without destroying each other, from the shelter of their roles (bureaucratic or feudal) then they must rationally

65

accept that there shall be an arbitrator to regulate such en-
counters. But who, it has been asked, *are* these individualists
who confront each other with such hostility? And the com-
monest answer has been: the bourgeoisie. The horrors of
Leviathan have been thought to be a brilliant image of capitalist
civilization.

Yet Hobbes fascinates us because he cannot convincingly be
tied down to so local a role. When William Golding wrote
in his novel, *Lord of the Flies*, an account of the degeneration
into barbarism of a group of English schoolboys cast away on
a tropical island, critics were quick to observe the connexion
with Hobbes. But *Leviathan* is equally convincing as an
account of the behaviour of the great powers on the international scene. It is a challenge to Marxists, for if Hobbes is
right, then the withering away of the State Marx envisaged is
an idle dream. And it is a challenge to democrats, for it warns
us that our modern plural societies contain elements of a
divided sovereignty which cannot easily be held together.
The *Leviathan* is both philosophy and myth; and each element
nourishes the other.

BOOK-LIST

HOBBES, T., *Leviathan*, edited with an introduction by Michael
    Oakeshott (Oxford, 1957), or *Leviathan*, introduced and abridged
    by John Plamenatz (Fontana Paperbacks, 1963).
HOBBES, T., *The Citizen*, edited with an introduction by Sterling P.
    Lamprecht (New York, 1949).
HOBBES, T., *Body, Man and Citizen, A Selection of Hobbes's Writings*,
    edited and introduced by Richard Peters (London, 1962).
PETERS, R. S., *Hobbes* (Pelican Books, 1956).
STRAUSS, LEO, *The Political Philosophy of Hobbes* (Oxford, 1936;
    Phoenix Paperbacks, 1963).
MACPHERSON, C. B., *The Political Theory of Possessive Individualism*
    (Oxford Paperbacks, 1964).
MINTZ, SAMUEL, *The Hunting of Leviathan* (Cambridge, 1962).

5

JOHN LOCKE AND GOVERNMENT
BY CONSENT

MAURICE CRANSTON

THE common image of a philosopher is of a contemplative man, of one who spends his life in reading and meditation. John Locke was not this kind of man at all. He was active and versatile; by turns he had been a don, a doctor, diplomatist, a civil servant, an economist and a pamphleteer; in the later years of his life, as a celebrated author, he threw himself wholeheartedly into politics and public administration. And all this was done from something more than a sense of duty. It was one of Locke's central beliefs that a philosopher could never discover truth by sitting at home reading, brooding or talking to fellow intellectuals. For to cut oneself off from the world was to cut oneself off from experience, and experience was the only means by which one could ever learn anything.

It is part of the argument of Locke's chief work on metaphysics, his *Essay Concerning Human Understanding*, that men are born knowing nothing; they have no innate knowledge and no intuitive knowledge. What they know they learn through observation and reflection – in a word, experience. Our knowledge can never be absolute, or perfect, or incorrigible; but through the study of nature and reason, with the help of science and logic, we can diminish our ignorance; we can gain *some* understanding of the world, above all a practical understanding.

John Locke is sometimes called the founder of the Age of Reason. He was at any rate one of the founders of modern, western, bourgeois industrial civilization. Our world was made by scientists and statesmen, merchants and industrialists, and Locke was the first theorist to expound *their* view of life, to articulate their aspirations and justify their deeds. One thing which characterizes Locke's mind as a wholly modern one is the extent to which it differs from the medieval mind. The medieval mind was religious, imaginative, spiritual. It was preoccupied with thoughts of God and the life after death, and the unseen world. Locke's mind was earthbound, empirical, businesslike. He was a Christian in the sense that he believed Christ was the Messiah and that there was a life after death for the righteous. But he had no patience with any further religious dogmas. He had no belief in miracles, and he detested mysticism. He mistrusted people who had religious insights or visions of God or who kept thinking all the time about heaven and hell. He thought men's duty was to the world they lived in. He once said: 'Our portion lies only here in this little spot of earth, where we and all our concernments are shut up.'

Locke's teaching about the native ignorance of man had important implications for morals as well as religion. Many of Locke's predecessors thought that some sort of moral knowledge was innate in the human creation. Locke did not. What Nature had given all men – or which God had given all men – was a sentiment of self-love. The exercise of reason in combination with this sentiment of self-love produced morality. Locke summed up his moral teaching in these words –

Thus I think – it is a man's proper business to seek happiness and avoid misery. Happiness consists in what delights and contents the mind; misery is what disturbs, discomposes, or torments it. I will therefore make it my business to seek satisfaction and delight and avoid uneasiness and disquiet and to have as much of the one and as little of the other as may be. But here I must take care I mistake not, for if I prefer a short pleasure to a lasting one, it is plain I cross my own happiness.

Let me see then wherein consist the most lasting pleasures of this life; and that so far as I can observe is in these things –

First, Health, without which no sensual pleasure can have any relish. Secondly, Good Reputation, for that I find everybody is pleased with, and the want of it a torment. Thirdly, Knowledge, for the little knowledge that I have, I find I would not sell at any rate, nor part with for any pleasure. Fourthly, Doing Good, I find the well-cooked meat I ate today does now no more delight me; nay, I am diseased after a full meal. The perfumes I smelt yesterday now no more affect me with any pleasure. But the good turn I did yesterday, a year, seven years hence, continues still to please me as often as I reflect upon it. Fifthly, the expectation of eternal and incomprehensible happiness in another world also carries a constant pleasure with it. If then I will faithfully pursue that happiness I propose to myself, whatever pleasure offers itself to me, I must carefully look that it cross not any of those five great and constant pleasures mentioned.

The reference to eternal life is the only feature of that *credo* which can be called Christian. But it is still an important part of it, and one must never forget that while Locke stripped the Christian faith down to its barest essentials, he clung to that minimal creed with the utmost assurance. He did not see any antithesis between New Testament ethics and his own ethics. The end in both was happiness. Loving one's neighbour and otherwise obeying the precepts of the Saviour was a way to happiness. The reason for doing what Christ said was not simply that Christ had said it, but because doing those things increased one's own satisfaction. There was no need to ask why anyone should desire satisfaction, because all men were impelled by their native self-love to do so. Wrong-doing was thus for Locke a sign of ignorance. People did not realize that long-term pleasures could usually only be bought at the cost of short-term pleasures. Folly drove them to destroy their own happiness. If people were enlightened, they would be good; if they were prudent, instead of hasty, they would get what they really wanted.

There is something perhaps naïve, rather specious, even commonplace about this system of ethics. Indeed one must say about Locke generally that he was in many ways very ordinary as a thinker; but his was an inspired ordinariness, a prophetic common sense. A lot of things which we take for granted today were new and remarkable when he first said them.

He was born in 1632, the eldest son of a small country lawyer in Somerset. He was ten years old when the Civil

War broke out, and his father fought on the side of the Parliament against the King. The Parliamentary victory enabled Locke to become a pupil first at the then best school in the country, Westminster, and later, the then best Oxford college, Christ Church. Locke was a scholarly youth, and when he had taken his degree he was invited to remain at Oxford as a lecturer in classics.

He was twenty-eight when King Charles II returned to England to occupy the throne; and Locke, like the majority of Englishmen, rejoiced in the Restoration. The Parliamentary victory in the Civil War had led to a military dictatorship; Oxford itself had been several times purged in the name of freedom; and although Locke had been brought up in a staunchly anti-royalist home, experience had made him the most eager of monarchists. At the time of the Restoration he wrote —

I find that a general freedom is but a general bondage, that the popular assentors of public liberty are the greatest engrossers of it too ... All the freedom I can wish my country or myself is to enjoy the protection of those laws which the prudence and providence of our ancestors established and the happy return of his Majesty has restored. There is no one can have a greater veneration for authority than I.

These last words have an ironical edge to them in view of Locke's subsequent activities as a political pamphleteer and theorist. For it was Locke's destiny to be remembered as the champion not of authority but of liberty: remembered, indeed, as a champion of armed rebellion. But twenty years and more were to pass between the restoration of Charles II and Locke's avowal of these radical policies. In the first few years after the Restoration Locke was preoccupied with his own worries. He did not want to become a clergyman, though at that time practically every tutor at an Oxford or Cambridge college was obliged to be in Holy Orders. So he tried diplomacy; but gave it up. Then he took to medicine, but he could not persuade the university to give him the full Doctor's degree. He also took up general science, a subject which was then entirely new to Oxford, and no part of the official studies, but which was pursued, as a hobby, by a small group of scholars in Robert Boyle's private laboratory.

The thing which did most to set Locke on the road to revolutionary liberalism was a chance meeting at Oxford with a politician – a statesman, as he later became – then Lord Ashley afterwards the first Earl of Shaftesbury. Lord Shaftesbury persuaded Locke to leave Oxford, and join his household in London as physician, friend and general adviser. Shaftesbury was the founder of the Whig Party in Parliament. What he stood for, in the first instance, was religious toleration. The majority in Parliament at the time of Charles II's Restoration wanted to force every Englishman into the Church of England by means of harsh penalties. Shaftesbury believed that everyone should be left alone to worship as he pleased. Shaftesbury was an innovator. His motive for wanting religious freedom was largely practical. The great passion of his life was trade. He was the real pioneer of British commercial imperialism. He saw more clearly than any of his contemporaries that vast fortunes could be made if commercial enterprise was freed from medieval fetters, and bold advances made into overseas markets and sources of supply. Religious toleration had enabled the Dutch merchants to thrive. Shaftesbury believed that if the English put an end to their religious squabbles they too could build up a vast commercial empire not only as great as that of Holland but as great as that of Rome.

Shaftesbury was not, of course, the only man with imperial ambitions in seventeenth-century Europe: there was also the King of France, Louis XIV. As the years went by, and Shaftesbury realized what Louis was doing, he grew to hate and fear France. This mounting Francophobia had two important effects on the line he pursued in party politics. First it made him ever more bitterly opposed to the Church of Rome, which was, he believed, subservient to French imperialist ambitions. Secondly it turned him against his King, Charles II, because Charles II became both the pensioner of Louis XIV and a secret Catholic. Thus Shaftesbury found himself advocating both war with France and the suppression of Catholicism in England. Locke was the man who helped him formulate the principles by which this party line was justified. Indeed, the whole of Locke's political philosophy was called into being by the exigencies of the times he lived through, and the circumstances of his being in the household of the opposition leader.

The first contradiction – or seeming contradiction – that Locke was called upon to resolve in Shaftesbury's policy was that of urging at the same time religious toleration and the suppression of Catholics or 'Papists', as he liked to call them. Locke's defence of this policy is shrewdly argued –

> The whole trust, power and authority of the civil ruler is vested in him for no other purpose but to be made use of for the good, preservation, and peace of men in that society over which he is set ... The civil ruler hath nothing to do with the good of men's souls or their concernment in another life, but is ordained and entrusted with his power only for the quiet and comfortable living of all men in society, one with another. Any religious opinion should therefore be tolerated so long as the profession of it does not undermine the security of the realm. Papists cannot be tolerated because their opinions are absolutely destructive to all governments except the Pope's. Papists, moreover, are not to enjoy toleration because when they have power, they think themselves bound to deny it to others.

Locke never altered his opinion on this subject. All his life he continued to recommend toleration of every religious sect except the Papists: and he always gave the same reasons for it – that the Papists put loyalty to the Pope above loyalty to the English constitution; and that they denied, where they had power, the religious liberty of others. In the year 1681, Shaftesbury's hostility to Catholicism brought him into bitter conflict with Charles II. Shaftesbury did not so much mind Charles's own leanings towards Catholicism: he knew the King was too worldly a man to become fanatically religious. What Shaftesbury feared was the succession of Charles's brother, James, an open and earnest Papist, and the legitimate heir to the throne. When Charles refused to exclude his brother from the right to the succession, Shaftesbury organized a rebel army and called the nation to revolt. The move proved abortive and Shaftesbury fled to Holland, where soon afterwards he died. Locke followed him to Amsterdam.

While Locke was in exile, the Catholic James II succeeded Charles II on the throne of England. His rule proved every bit as bad as Shaftesbury said it would be. James II tried to impose the Catholic faith on Englishmen, he dispensed with Parliament and he took away many of the ordinary citizen's ancient rights and privileges. In the end, he drove the nation so hard that the English rose in arms to expel him from the throne, and to set up a Protestant constitutional monarch in his place. This was the 'Glorious Revolution' of 1688 which put King William and Queen Mary on the throne. Locke, who returned to England when James fled, became known as the philosopher of the Glorious Revolution – by reason of the fact that he published his *Two Treatises of Government* within a few months of those stirring events.

Now this was a work about which Locke himself was extraordinarily secretive. A few days before he died, in 1704, he wrote a codicil to his will naming the *Two Treatises of Government* among his anonymous works for the benefit of the Bodleian Library. But this is the only time we know him to have acknowledged it. At other times he denied having written the book, or evaded questions on the subject, and sought to conceal his authorship even from his closest friends and collaborators.

There is no question of Locke's being ashamed of the book. Far from it. In a letter to a distant cousin who wanted a reading list of books on the theory of the constitution, Locke recommended, together with Aristotle's *Politics* and Hooker's *Ecclesiastical Polity* 'a book entitled *Two Treatises of Government*'. The same recommendation is made in Locke's *Some Thoughts Concerning Reading and Study for a Gentleman*. In writing to his cousin Locke recommended the book especially for its treatment of one particular problem: 'property', he said, 'I have nowhere found more clearly explained'. In both cases, Locke referred to the book and praised it as if it had

73

been written by somebody else, somebody he did not know.

Several wrong ideas about Locke's *Two Treatises* may still need to be corrected. First there is the idea, once universally established, that the book was written to justify the Glorious Revolution of 1688. Now it is true that Locke was, to some extent, concerned to justify that Revolution. In the 'Preface to the Reader' Locke wrote –

These papers I hope are sufficient to establish the throne of our great Restorer, our present King William, to make good his title in the consent of the people, which being the only one of lawful governments, he has more fully and clearly than any Prince in Christendom; I hope these papers are sufficient also to justify to the world the people of England, whose love of their just and natural rights, with their revolution to preserve them, saved the Nation when it was on the very brink of slavery and ruin.

This famous passage has led some historians to speak of Locke's *Two Treatises* as a *pièce d'occasion* prompted by the Glorious Revolution. But this is a mistake. The fact that Locke's book, being published when it was, did serve in the event to make a case for William III, does not mean that it was written with that intention. In fact, one has only to read Locke's Preface carefully to realize that the book must have had a longer and more complex history; for Locke's first words to the Reader are –

Thou hast here the beginning and the end of a discourse concerning government; what Fate has otherwise disposed of the Papers that should have filled up the middle, and were more than all the rest, 'tis not worth while to tell thee.

It now seems clear that the book was written something like ten years before the Glorious Revolution. And this is a much more interesting date. The book remains a *pièce d'occasion*, as the textbooks call it; only it becomes a piece of a different occasion, something written, not to justify a revolution which had already taken place, but to set forth the argument for a revolution which was being planned. It does not belong to the settled years of the reign of William and Mary, but to the perilous years of Shaftesbury's Protestant Plot against

Charles II. The *Two Treatises of Government*, when it was first written, was a seditious and inflammatory document.

Now to speak of Locke's *Treatises* as a polemical tract is not to diminish in any way its claim to be a work of philosophy. Much of the best political philosophy, from the *Republic* of Plato to J. S. Mill's *Essay on Liberty*, has been written by men who were disturbed about the way the world was going, and who wanted urgently to change its direction. Locke's work is both theoretical and didactic. He passes from the particular question of his own duty to his own king to the general question of any man's duty to any ruler, and so to the problems of obligation and of sovereignty at the highest level of abstraction. If Locke's dilemma was peculiar to his own time and place, his method of dealing with it entailed the working out of principles of universal validity; it is this which makes the *Treatises* an important and timely document still in 1965. The fundamental problems Locke deals with are still with us. One key word in this whole book is 'consent'. The idea that the authority of a king or other ruler rested on the consent of the people he ruled was a controversial one in the seventeenth century. King James and the other Stuarts believed that their royal authority derived from God: indeed the Divine Right of Kings was a widely accepted belief throughout Europe. Hobbes had attacked this doctrine, but Hobbes was too bold and extreme a writer to be popular, and it was Locke more than any other theorist who overthrew belief in the Rights of Kings.

At the same time Locke followed Hobbes in trying to put forward what he regarded as a scientific basis for political obligation. He began by asking: 'why do governments exist at all?' He decided that there must once have been a time when there was no government on earth, no political societies; and when all men had lived in a state of anarchy, or what Locke called a 'state of nature'. This state of natural anarchy had proved intolerable: for where every man was a law unto himself, life could not be orderly, peaceful and predictable. The weak had no protection against the strong: and the strong themselves were in perpetual fear of their rivals. So men had come together and formed political societies: they had entrusted sovereigns or civil rulers with power over them. It is important to stress the word 'entrusted': for Locke did not believe that the authority of the civil ruler was ever absolute – it was a trust, and therefore revocable. All sovereigns in the world owed their power to the original social contracts made at the dawn of history. Consent was thus their only title to rule –

The liberty of Man in society is to be under no other legislative power but that established by consent in the commonwealth, nor under the dominion of any will, or restraint of any law, but what that legislation shall enact, according to the trust put in it. Freedom for man under government is not for every one to do as he lists but to have a standing rule to live by, common to everyone of that society, and made by the legislative power erected in it; to have a liberty to follow his own will in all things where the Rule prescribes not, and not to be subject to the inconstant, uncertain, unknown, arbitrary Will of another man.

This doctrine of consent as the only basis of political obligation meant that a society had the right to rid itself of a ruler who betrayed the trust reposed in him; the right, in a word, to rebellion. But how was one to decide at what point a ruler could be held to have betrayed his trust? Locke's answer was that a ruler betrayed his trust when he forsook government according to settled processes of law in favour of 'inconstant, uncertain, unknown, and arbitrary government'. James II had done this: he had put himself above the law: he had forfeited the people's trust –

... whenever the legislators endeavour to take away or destroy the property of the people, or to reduce them to slavery under arbitrary power, they put themselves into a state of war with the people, who are thereupon absolved from any further obedience, and are left to the common refuge, which God hath provided for all men against force and violence – resistance.

Locke's principle of resistance had implications that he himself did not entirely perceive, but which his successors were swift to seize upon. Locke himself was, like Shaftesbury, an imperialist. He believed it was quite just that Ireland and the American colonies, for example, should be subject to the King of England. But the people who lived in those colonies came in time to feel that as they themselves had no real share in the political life of England, they must withhold their consent from the continued sovereignty of the English crown over their territory. If their consent was withdrawn, where was then the title of the English crown to rule them? On Locke's principles it did not exist: and as the English continued to force their king's authority in the colonies, the colonists felt they were justified in taking up arms. In France Locke's principles were pressed to even fuller extremes. The French decided that the principle of consent carried the right not only to replace a tyrannical king but to get rid of the entire constitution and try to reshape society afresh.

Locke was thus the intellectual pioneer of the age of Revolution as well as of the age of Reason. But Locke himself was much too cautious a man to have approved of what was done in, for example, the French Revolution or the Russian Revolution. In the words I have already quoted from the preface to the *Two Treatises of Government*, Locke describes the English as acting in 1688 to *preserve* their rights. Their Revolution is thus represented as a *conservative* movement – not a movement to introduce a new and better society, but to recover ancient rights that had been taken away by the usurper, the unlawful James II. Locke, significantly, calls King William the great *Restorer* – not the great Innovator. Locke's revolutionary creed is far removed from the left-wing ideologies of the French and the Russian revolutionaries, who did not wish to regain what was lost, but to achieve something that had never been enjoyed before. Locke would never have approved of revolution as a means to initiate an egalitarian, socialistic, or other ideal republic. He believed in revolution only where it was necessary to regain men's elementary, natural rights.

I have said Locke repudiated the Stuart notion of the Divine Right of Kings. What he put in its place was a modernized notion of the Natural Rights of Man. Locke believed

77

the one thing worth fighting for was this. The Rights of Man do not constitute the whole framework of law. They are simply those things which are universal and essential to all men: the things without which life is intolerable. Locke is thus the pioneer of the kind of thinking about liberty which finds expression in the Universal Declaration of Human Rights proclaimed by the United Nations in 1948. But when Locke spoke of Rights he did not think of 'ideals'.

Indeed idealism of any kind was entirely alien to his businesslike teaching. The Rights of Man were not ends to which Locke thought man might aspire: they were the basic human needs which every ruler should concede on pain of expulsion. Locke summed up these Rights of Man as Life, Liberty and Property: and the critic might reasonably wish to know what each of those abstract words is supposed to mean in concrete terms. By the Rights to life and liberty Locke meant that no ruler could be allowed to retain his office if he killed or imprisoned innocent men, or if he allowed any man, unpunished, to attack another man's person: by the Right to property, Locke meant that no ruler could be allowed to retain his office if he seized any man's property, other than by a proper system of taxation; or if he allowed any man, unpunished, to seize the property of another.

The enforcement of these rights entailed, Locke argued, certain necessary institutions: a representative assembly of taxpayers to authorize taxation, for example; and an independent system of judiciary, to ensure that no innocent man was ever penalized by the State. Some newly formed States of the present day have tried to dispense with such institutions: and in doing so, they have forsaken liberty and enthroned dictators. Locke denies the name of law to the enactments of dictators –

For laws not being made for themselves, but to be by their execution the bonds of the society to keep every part of the body politic in its due place and function, when that totally ceases, the government visibly ceases, and the people become a confused multitude without order or connexion. Where there is no longer the administration of justice for the protection of men's rights, nor any remaining power within the community to direct the force or provide for the necessities of the public, there is certainly no government left.

In these and like cases where the government is dissolved, the people are at liberty to provide for themselves by erecting a new legislative, differing from the other by the change of persons or form or both as they shall find it most for their safety and good. For the society can never by the fault of another lose the native and original right it has to preserve itself, which can only be done by a settled legislative, and a fair and impartial execution of the laws made by it.

In the preface to most printed editions of Locke's *Letter for Toleration* there is a sentence which reads 'Absolute liberty, just and true liberty, equal and impartial liberty is the thing we stand in need of'. These words are not Locke's. Locke wrote the *Letter for Toleration* in Latin, and the plea for absolute liberty was added by William Popple, a Unitarian friend of Locke's, who translated the text into English.

Locke did *not* believe in absolute liberty any more than he believed in absolute knowledge: his attitude towards the one was on all fours with his attitude towards the other. In the capacity of a pure philosopher, Locke set out to demonstrate that human knowledge was bound to be limited; and indeed that it could not be extended to the fullest possible limits unless the existence of those limits was fully understood. The way to pursue fruitful inquiries was, in the first place, to avoid futile inquiries. Hence the seeming paradox of Locke's attempt in his *Essay Concerning Human Understanding* to show how much men can know by showing how little they can know.

Locke's political philosophy is argued along the same lines as his pure philosophy. He sets out to show how much liberty men can have by pointing out the limits that must be set on men's liberty. The limits that are set on liberty are dictated by the nature of political societies as such. One man's freedom stops short at the point where it would injure another man's freedom. Hence freedom in political society is freedom under law. Far from being absolute, it is most precisely circumscribed.

The great advantage, however, of being quite clear about the limitation of freedom is that it enables men to see exactly how much freedom they can have: it shows them what is possible and what is worth striving for. Locke set men on the path to the greatest possible political liberty by the method he used to set them on the path to the greatest possible scientific knowledge – by teaching them the impossibility of the absolute.

BOOK-LIST

LOCKE, JOHN, *Two Treatises of Government*, edited by Peter Laslett (Cambridge, 1960).

LOCKE, JOHN, *The Second Treatise of Civil Government* and *A Letter Concerning Toleration*, edited by J. W. Gough (Oxford, 1946).

LOCKE, JOHN, *Essays on the Law of Nature*, edited by W. von Leyden (Oxford, 1954).

Among books concerning John Locke are the following –

COX, RICHARD H., *Locke on War and Peace* (Oxford, 1960).

CRANSTON, MAURICE, *John Locke: a Biography* (London, 1957).

GOUGH, J. W., *John Locke's Political Philosophy* (Oxford, 1950).

O'CONNOR, D. J., *John Locke* (Penguin paperback, 1952).

6

MONTESQUIEU AND THE VARIETIES
OF POLITICAL EXPERIENCE

G. C. MORRIS

EVEN two centuries after his death (on 10 February 1755)
the figure of Charles Louis de Secondat, Baron de Montesquieu, remains enigmatic. We are not yet agreed upon his
stature, his originality, his importance. He has been looked
upon as a radical, almost revolutionary, humanitarian and
also as a subtle, if critical upholder of feudal institutions. He
has been hailed as a forerunner both of Burke and of Robes-
pierre. He was formerly over-praised as a systematic philosopher and thought to be offering men a panacea. He is now
more often praised as one who distrusted the universal
application of any formula or system, who could detect the
intricacies and complexities of social problems, who had a sure
eye for social or even moral relativity. He has enjoyed a
succès d'estime as at least a pioneer and perhaps the inventor of
scientific sociology, although eminent sociologists (among
them the great Durkheim) have condemned him for having
failed to be properly scientific or systematic, for being too
little of a materialist or too little of a determinist, for being
inconsistent or inaccurate, for basing his sociology on un-
stated metaphysical assumptions or for using sociological
observations in a purely anecdotal, almost frivolous manner,
to point a moral or adorn a tale.

Such critics are hardly original, for it was Dr Johnson who
once observed that whenever Montesquieu 'wants to support
a strange opinion, he quotes you the practice of Japan or of
some other distant country. To support polygamy he tells
you of the island of Formosa, where there are ten women
born for one man.' And it was Macaulay who wrote of him

that, 'If nothing established by authentic testimony can be racked or chipped to suit his Procrustean hypothesis, he puts up with some monstrous fable about Siam, or Bantam, or Japan, told by writers compared with whom Lucian and Gulliver were veracious, liars by a double right, as travellers and as Jesuits.'

From the beginning opinions have differed about the nature of Montesquieu's message. D'Alembert praised him for being 'less occupied with laws that have been made than with those which ought to be made', whereas to Condorcet he seemed 'more occupied with finding the reasons for what is than with seeking what ought to be'. Montesquieu would have enjoyed the joke and indeed predicted it, for he said that he expected to be more approved of than actually read. The irony of this is that, of all writers who are in fact little read, none is more eminently readable. Perhaps Montesquieu is too unruffled and urbane, too extraverted and eupeptic to appear a genius. We expect genius to be neurotic, to have a thorn in the flesh or at least a bee in the bonnet, to be like Hobbes or Marx or Rousseau. A genius should not say, like Montesquieu, that he had never experienced any sorrow which an hour's reading did not dissipate. Perhaps, too, a genius should not use a style so limpid and so witty that it is bound to strike duller minds as being inconsistent with profundity.

Montesquieu led the serene sheltered life of a grandee, most of it within his well-appointed library in the *château* of La Brède, near Bordeaux. The library measured sixty feet by forty. Some four years on the Grand Tour (nearly half of them with his friend Lord Chesterfield in England), some visits to Paris, and twelve years' part-time work as hereditary magistrate (*Président à Mortier*) in the *parlement* of Bordeaux represent his only first-hand contacts with the world outside.

He had a passionate admiration for his fellow Gascon Montaigne; he had the Gascon's traditional delight in gaiety and wit; and he was not above an elegant salaciousness in certain of his minor works. But his parents were aristocrats with an old-fashioned gravity and a strong, semi-religious sense of social responsibility. At the hour of his birth (18 January 1689) a beggar happened to call at the castle gates and was solemnly appointed godfather to the child, to remind him throughout life that the poor were his brothers. Montesquieu did remember.

Early in life he attempted certain amateurish scientific experiments – on the renal gland, on echo and on transparency in bodies. But he gave up because he was growing short-sighted, and a little short of patience. Montesquieu was never truly scientific any more. His knowledge was encyclopedic but it came from books. Like his modern counterpart, Sir James Frazer, he did no 'field-work'. This, possibly, weakens his claim to have discovered the scientific laws of politics. Many of his facts are carefully selected to confirm his opinions; they are seldom studied for their own sake unless he thinks them entertaining. He is not always concerned with what savages or orientals are really like. They are sometimes used as sticks with which to belabour the stupidities of his own western world. All that we learn, for instance, of the natives of Louisiana is that 'when they wish for some fruit, they cut down the tree and then pick the fruit; such is the character of despotic government'. The scientist in Montesquieu could not overcome the satirist. In a sense he never recovered from the success of his early work, *Les Lettres Persanes* (1721), an enchanting satirical coruscation in which two Persian travellers gaze with quizzical insouciance at western Christendom. From it is descended a whole literary *genre* – Voltaire's *L'Ingénu* and Johnson's *Rasselas*, Goldsmith's *Citizen of the World* and Lowes Dickinson's *Letters From John Chinaman*.

Les Lettres Persanes were among the intellectual first-fruits of the expansion of Europe. From travel-books like Chardin's or Tavernier's, or from Jesuit 'relations', European thinkers were learning not only of the noble savage but of enlightened Shahs or Moguls and of the sage Chinese. Montesquieu's teaching, elaborated in his masterpiece *de L'Esprit des Lois* (1748), is that human institutions can and should vary, that there is more than one way of being civilized, that circumstances alter cases, that different climates and traditions will require different modes of government, that a country's laws need to be *en rapport* with the local traditions, that 'nature' and 'reason' do not always and everywhere demand the same laws and the same reforms.

Yet Montesquieu was no mere empiricist; for no eighteenth-century intellectual could abandon all belief in the universal, self-evident truths of 'nature' and of 'reason'. And so he was apt to say that an aristocracy is hereditary 'by nature', that slavery is intrinsically bad 'in its nature', or that torture 'is not by its own nature necessary'. At one moment he is about to discuss the possible utility of torture to a despot, but recoils with the exclamation: 'I hear the voice of Nature crying out against me.' Nor would he admit that what is just or unjust is simply what the laws of any given state decree. To say so was 'to say that, until someone has drawn a circle, its radii are not all equal'. Montesquieu was critical of Venice, the only complete republic he had seen; but 'republican virtue' remained for him an axiom, on *a priori* grounds and because he read of it in Plutarch.

Montesquieu's axioms and laws of nature are half-way between the descriptive and the prescriptive. He is full of what might be called, according to taste, either logical absurdities or saving inconsistencies. He comes near to making an 'ought' statement follow from an 'is'. Men do in fact pursue certain aims; therefore it is right for them to do so. The 'done thing' is done because it should be done. Man is in fact born free and reasonable; therefore we ought to see that he remains so. Montesquieu steers indeed a middle course between fact and theory, between particular and general. He sought after general rules, for he supposed that he was founding a new science of society. But, because of his temperament and because of his intellectual honesty, it was on the exception and the complication that he liked to dwell. He was certainly no doctrinaire and he certainly did not over-simplify. He held that there were absolutes, that justice and liberty were always good, but he knew that the roads leading to them could be various and winding. He knew that the basic problem in ethics is to account equally for the remarkable amount both of agreement and of disagreement over moral issues which in fact occurs.

He believed in truths that were fixed and knowable but also that it was inhumane, dangerous and perhaps impossible to eradicate long-standing error. If men were free, they must have the freedom to be wrong. He was well aware that the easiest way to promote truth was through a despotism, but he also thought it to be of all ways the most pernicious. He knew that despotism could be benevolent but that it remained despotism, and therefore hateful, none the less. Although he loved liberty with passion, he had no illusions as to the risks, the sacrifices, the agonizing choices, the delicate and difficult equilibria, the social and political elasticity, the delays, the compromises, the acceptance of give and take that liberty involves. His faith in liberty, in what would now be called the 'open society', was founded perhaps on the belief, deep-seated in all eighteenth-century savants, that private interests did ultimately harmonize, that, through the benevolent dispensation of Nature, men could be rogues or frauds individually but decent or honest in the mass.

As a sociologist Montesquieu again takes a middle way between particular and general, for he is not greatly interested in what some individual ruler can do for his individual subjects, nor yet in 'Man' with a big M. He is interested in groups of men as such, in societies rather than Society, in men as they are made by varying and changing environments and institutions. He is also trying to discover the permanent laws governing such changes. And he is trying to eliminate mere contingency, to find a way of making government accident-proof. But, although he is concerned both with causes and with effects, he is little concerned with the historical process in itself. He wants to know what men are and the basic reasons why, but not in any detail how they became so. He lacked the historical approach of his near contemporary Vico. For Montesquieu societies were natural biological organisms. Their origins and basic purposes were self-evident and required little explanation. What mattered and what needed explanation was their variation. The causation of society was simple and purely material; the causation of social variety was something much more complex, much more to do with morals and much more interesting. Besides, it was the function of education and of enlightened government to see that moral factors prevailed over the material. Only with savages is the physical predominant. Montesquieu believed that societies not only varied but could and should progress, but he was realist enough to know that progress was not likely to be rapid. 'Government', he said, 'is a blunt file working slowly and arriving slowly at its end.'

The sobriety and caution of Montesquieu's approach is apt to conceal from us his revolutionary impact on his own age. He caused men to think that there were laws governing society which were no less discoverable than the laws of physics, that human affairs need no longer be regarded as a branch of theology rather than a branch of science. He also broke away from the age-old classical analysis of constitutions, an analysis in which the determining factor is what men and how many of them do the governing. Montesquieu ignored the long-standing classification in terms of monarchy, aristocracy, democracy – and produced a new one of his own, in which governments were seen as despotisms, as monarchies (meaning limited or constitutional monarchies) or as republics. These were distinguished from one another not by analysis in terms of class or number but in a much subtler and more truly sociological way. Montesquieu had seen that what mattered was not so much who wielded power but how power was wielded, that laws and constitutions mattered far less than the informing 'principle' or spirit, the tone or mood, the habits or values, the dynamic or ethos, the morale or rationale which made them work ill or well. Aristotle had said much of this centuries before but in Montesquieu's day it needed to be said again.

In despotism the ruling principle was 'fear', in monarchy 'honour' and in republics 'virtue'. By monarchy Montesquieu meant feudal monarchy working as it ought to work, the society of aristocratic prestige and aristocratic responsibility, the world in which *noblesse oblige* – perhaps the world in which Montesquieu had himself grown up, that of the feudal *château* at La Brède. The most valuable part of his historical researches was that which threw light on the origins of French feudal law; in fact Montesquieu did much to put the concept of feudalism permanently upon the map of history. But he had done something of perhaps even wider significance, for his account of the society in which 'honour' sets the tone was the fullest description since Homer's of what anthropologists would now call a 'shame culture'. In such a culture, wrote Montesquieu, 'men's actions are not judged as good but as fine, not as just but as glorious, not as rational but as magnificent'.

By a 'republic' Montesquieu did not mean democracy. He meant that kind of society, whether oligarchic or relatively democratic, in which the prime social value is 'virtue'. This was a quality nearer in meaning to high morale than to good morals: it is not unrelated to what Machiavelli called *virtù*. The question Montesquieu is most apt to ask is not whether a society promotes general moral goodness but whether it does in fact promote whatever it is that the society in question has chosen to promote. In other words, is it a viable society, can it go on being the kind of society it would like to be? And a republic, according to Montesquieu, though not necessarily more moral, has more of this stamina or capacity to survive than has any other type of State. Unfortunately republican 'virtue' is held to be something of a lost secret known only to the ancients. For 'moderns' the most viable government is now monarchy tempered by a robust, honourable and responsible nobility, and tempered also by the rule of law.

On the causes of a social ethos Montesquieu is sometimes superficial, attributing too much to climate – although by 'climate' he often means the whole of man's environment. Here Montesquieu comes close to the theories outlined by Bodin nearly two centuries earlier, although, unlike Bodin, Montesquieu excludes astrological influence over human affairs. All he really claims is that: 'Man, in so far as he is a physical being, is, like other bodies, governed by unchanging laws.' And Montesquieu refines this by explaining that different physical environments give rise to different needs, which in turn produce different modes of life; and it is 'these different modes of life which have formed the different kinds of law'. Climate is only one factor among many; and it is the factor which, although first in point of time, is by no means the most important except among the least civilized of peoples –

Various things govern mankind – climate, religion, laws, maxims of government, past precedents, morals, customs; from all of these is formed a resultant general ethos. In proportion as, within each society, one of these factors operates with greater force, the other causes to that degree give way to it. Nature and climate reign almost alone over savages; manners govern the Chinese; laws tyrannize over Japan; morals formerly set the tone in Sparta; maxims of government combined with ancient traditions produced it in Rome.

Nevertheless Montesquieu can argue, whether cynically or fancifully we cannot be quite sure, that –

The concept of metempsychosis is adapted to the climate of India; the excessive heat burns up all the pasture; there is little enough grazing for the cattle; one can easily run short of them for tillage; the cattle have a very moderate rate of increase; they are subject to many a disease; a religious injunction which keeps them alive is therefore a great convenience for the country's government.

But he was well aware that, as soon as the primitive stages of social evolution have been passed, all sorts of immaterial causes begin to operate and to build up a complex and subtle superstructure in which the relevant impulses are psychological and moral. And Montesquieu can be profound and penetrating on these psychological factors, on the symptoms of good or bad morale, of vigour or corruption in the body politic.

As he surveyed the continent of Europe Montesquieu feared that 'monarchy' was breaking down and might well be going the way of the ancient republics. Despotism on the oriental model, just because it provides so many easy answers and saves people so much trouble, because allegedly it 'gets things done', might be the coming thing. But when he looked north-west the land was brighter. Every sophisticated thinker in the eighteenth century had some kind of belief in some kind of noble savage. Montesquieu's noble savage was not the Huron or the Chinaman; nor was it the ancient Roman or the ancient Teuton, both of whom he somewhat romanticized. It was the Englishman.

What Montesquieu admired most in England was her high morale, which he connected with the constitutional safeguards that preserved her from corruption, from the despot's caprice and from demagogic irresponsibility. From his observation of England he imported the new word 'constitutionalism' into the French language. Montesquieu was impressed not only by the vigour of English political life and by the prosperity of the English economy. He found in English high society something peculiarly sympathetic, for he was himself the French equivalent of a Whig mandarin. England, moreover, seemed to him to have preserved something of the lost 'virtue' of a classical republic and at the same time to have retained the aristocratic 'honour' and responsibility, the entrenched liberties and the supremacy of law which he associated with Teutonic feudal monarchy. 'If', he wrote, 'we take the trouble to read the admirable work of Tacitus on the institutions of the Germans, we shall realize that it is from them that the English have derived the pattern of their polity. This superb system was discovered in the forest.' This is not wholly absurd, for Montesquieu realized that England was the one country which had, in a sense, remained obstinately medieval, keeping her medieval freedoms just when other nations were becoming up to date by losing theirs.

As is well known, Montesquieu supposed that the English secret lay in the separation of powers – in the alleged keeping of legislative, executive and judicial functions quite apart. As is also well known, he got it wrong, although not quite so wrong as some critics have averred. Relying more on what he read in Locke and in Bolingbroke than on what he might have seen for himself, he underestimated the extent to which, in Walpole's England, the functions of government in fact interlocked and overlapped. When Montesquieu became in due course the idol of the founding fathers of the United States, he became, through the perpetuation of his error, partly responsible for some of the less happy features of the American Constitution. The Americans even swallowed Montesquieu's Teutonic myth and proposed at one time to engrave Hengist and Horsa on the Great Seal of the Republic.

Nevertheless, in the matter of the separated powers, Montesquieu had discerned at least a half-truth. With prophetic insight he had seen from afar something of what power might come to mean in a modern state. And he had seen that no mere sentiment, tradition, convention or ideology was strong enough to hold it in. One must set a thief to catch a thief; and nothing but power can put a brake on power – *Il faut que le pouvoir arrête le pouvoir*. Without this, totalitarianism follows. The current demand for an Ombudsman suggests that Montesquieu may not have been altogether wrong.

Montesquieu's greatness, however, does not lie in any one discovery, still less in any formula or dogma. His greatness is elusive because it is diffused. *De L'Esprit des Lois* is the most rewarding of all eighteenth-century books on politics and, in spite of much close reasoning and considerable formal unity, it is so because of its digressions. Montesquieu said himself that those who knew how to use digression were like people with long arms; 'they can reach further'. He is most worth reading because of his unending series of luminous, incisive *obiter dicta* on a hundred themes. Open him at random, and you may stumble on a theory of punishment which anticipates Beccaria's; he saw how brutal punishments will brutalize the public and how bad laws can make bad citizens. Or you may find him saying acutely that the law must presume men to be better than they are. This is no facile optimism; for Montesquieu is a political doctor, and a doctor must at least pretend that a disease is curable.

In one place Montesquieu anticipates the ideas of full employment and of the Welfare State –

A man is not poor because he possesses nothing but because he is out of work ... The artisan who has given his children his skill for their inheritance has left them a fortune which is multiplied in proportion to their number. The case is not the same with him who has ten acres of land to live on and divides them among his children.

And before long Montesquieu is saying –

The state owes to every citizen an assured subsistence, proper nourishment, suitable clothing, and a mode of life not incompatible with health. ... Wealth in a state implies large-scale industry. With such numerous branches of trade, it is inevitable that there will always be some which are depressed and in which the workers are in temporary need. Whenever this happens the state must provide them with immediate help – whether it be to prevent the people from suffering, or whether it be to prevent them from revolting.

The slightly cynical ambivalence is characteristic.

In another place Montesquieu ridicules the folly of an armaments-race and of excessive spending on defence –

A new disease is spreading over Europe; it has seized upon our princes and induces them to maintain an inordinate number of soldiers. The disease is attended by complications and it inevitably becomes contagious; for, as soon as one state increases what it calls its forces, the others immediately increase theirs; so that nothing is gained except mutual ruination. Each sovereign keeps mobilized all the divisions he would need if his subjects were threatened with extermination. And the name of 'peace' is given to this condition in which all compete against all. Thus Europe is rendered so bankrupt that, if private individuals found themselves in the situation of the three wealthiest powers of this part of the world, they would not have enough to live on. We remain poor though we have the wealth and commerce of the whole world; and soon, by dint of going in for soldiers, we shall all be nothing *but* soldiers. We shall in fact be like the Tartars. The greater princes, not content with buying up the troops of lesser powers, are looking everywhere for more alliances to pay for – almost always a sure means of throwing away their money. The result of such a state of affairs is the perpetual increase of taxation. And what prevents the finding of any remedy is that the state no longer relies on its income but wages war with its capital. It is no unheard-of thing for a government to mortgage its securities even in time of peace and to employ – for bringing about its own ruin – what are called extraordinary measures – measures indeed so extraordinary that they could hardly have entered the dreams of the wildest young spendthrift.

It is difficult to remember that those words were written over two centuries ago.

Elsewhere, in a passage of *Les Lettres Persanes*, Montesquieu may have been more prophetic still –

Ever since the invention of gunpowder ... I continually tremble in case men should, in the end, uncover some secret which would provide a short way of abolishing mankind, of annihilating peoples and nations in their entirety.

Montesquieu can often be prophetic. He even foreshadows Rousseau's moralizing of the State when he writes that 'Liberty consists only in the power to do what we ought to will, and in not being made to do what we ought not to will.' Libery for Montesquieu was of course no crude anarchic thing. It was desirable mainly because men have to be supposed reasonable beings, although, even if they were not, to trust them with liberty would be the best means of inducing rationality among them. In any case, says Montesquieu, men 'only do well what they do freely.'

Montesquieu is at his best where he can be ironical and compassionate at once. Voltaire, who was jealous of him, did not excel him in this vein. He has an unforgettable chapter on the burning of little Jewish girls by the Inquisition. He calls it 'the most futile passage ever written. When one tries to prove things so self-evident, one is certain to be unconvincing.' To persecute Judaism, he argues, is to persecute 'the pardonable error of supposing that God still loves what He once loved in the past'. If the Inquisitors cannot be truly Christian, let them at least behave like human beings, 'guided only by the faint light of justice which Nature has given us'. They have little excuse, since they 'live in an age in which the light of Nature is brighter than it has ever been before'. But if posterity is ever tempted to think of eighteenth-century Europeans as civilized, 'You', cries Montesquieu to the Inquisitors, 'will be cited to prove that they were barbarous.'

Montesquieu has a passage, perhaps even more trenchant, on Negro slavery. He pretends, with mordant sarcasm, to defend it –

The peoples of Europe, having exterminated the peoples of America, were bound to enslave those of Africa. How else could they have brought such vast areas under cultivation? [Again] ... sugar would be far too dear if the plant producing it was not cultivated by slaves. [Besides] ... it is virtually impossible to feel compassion for people who are black from head to foot and who have such flattened noses. [And] ... how could it have come into the mind of God, who is a very wise being, to put a soul, still less a good soul, into an all-black body? It is so natural to regard colour as constituting the essence of being human that the Asiatics, who manufacture eunuchs, always deprive negroes of any kinship they may have with ourselves – in a yet more signal fashion. We can test the importance of colour in the skin by reference to that of hair which among the Egyptians (the best philosophers of the world) was a matter of such great moment that they always put to death any red-headed men who fell into their hands. One proof that negroes lack all common sense is that they attach more value to a glass necklace than to the gold which, among civilized peoples, is of such enormous consequence. It is impossible for us to suppose such creatures to be men because, if we did so, it would begin to be doubtful whether we ourselves can be Christians. Petty minds exaggerate excessively the injustice inflicted on the Africans; for, if it were such as they describe, would it not have occurred to the princes of Europe, who make so many useless agreements with one another, to make a general one in the cause of mercy and humanity?

This is an acid tone of voice which has, regrettably, gone out of fashion. It will also be seen that Montesquieu had not forgotten that he was 'brother to the poor'. There is perhaps something to be said, after all, for that eighteenth-century liberal 'enlightenment' which is now so unfashionable because it is so little understood and so little understood because, like Montesquieu himself, it is read so much at second-hand.

BOOK-LIST

There has been no English translation of *de L'Esprit des Lois* since that of THOMAS NUGENT (1766) which is not always elegant nor even always accurate. It is available (with slight emendations) in the Hafner Library of Classics (New York, 1949).

All translations given above are the author's.
The most recent books in English are –

BERLIN, SIR ISAIAH, British Academy Lecture on *Montesquieu*. *Proceedings of the British Academy*, Vol. XLI, 1955. A brilliant essay.

COURTNEY, C. P., *Montesquieu and Burke* (Oxford, 1963).

PLAMENATZ, J., *Man and Society*, Vol. I, Chapter 7 (London, 1963). Acute but perhaps over-critical.

SHACKLETON, R., *Montesquieu. A Critical Biography* (Oxford, 1961). Extremely scholarly. The definitive biography.

STARK, W., *Montesquieu as Pioneer of the Sociology of Knowledge* (London, 1960).

Among older works that are still useful are –

GRANT, A. J., Essay on Montesquieu in *The Social and Political Ideas of Some Great French Thinkers of the Age of Reason*. Ed. F. J. C. Hearnshaw (London, 1930).

VAUGHAN, C. E., *Studies in the History of Political Philosophy before and after Rousseau*, Vol. I, Chapter 5 (Manchester, 1925).

See also the relevant parts of –

CASSIRER, ERNST, *The Philosophy of the Enlightenment*, translated F. C. A. Koelln and J. P. Pettegrove (Boston, 1955).

HAZARD, PAUL, *European Thought in the Eighteenth Century. From Montesquieu to Lessing*, translated J. Lewis May (London, 1954).

MARTIN, KINGSLEY, *French Liberal Thought in the Eighteenth Century* (London, 1929; revised 1954).

7

ROUSSEAU AND THE GENERAL WILL

DAVID THOMSON

SOME political ideas are important, and remain important for a long time, because they seem to have come at a magic moment. Philosophers matter when they put forward ideas at just the right time – when old theories have worn thread-bare or reached a dead end – so that they put men's thinking on a new track, as it were, or on lines that may lead in un-expected directions. The ideas put forward at such a moment do not need to be new in themselves. They can be revivals of older half-forgotten ideas, or new combinations of familiar ideas that present them in a new light and suggest fresh con-clusions. It is to this last sort of philosophy that the theories of Jean-Jacques Rousseau belong.

The two books by which he is best remembered came out in the same year, 1762. One was *Émile*, a long and rather rambling philosophical romance about a new kind of educa-tion which would produce a truly 'Natural Man', uncorrupted by society yet able to fit into almost any way of life because he would be so self-contained. The other was the *Social Contract*, a much shorter and more closely argued book, about the right sort of State for free men. In the first sentence of the *Social Contract*, Rousseau made the link between the two books: 'I mean to inquire if, in the civil order, there can be any sure and legitimate rule of administration, men being taken as they are and laws as they might be.' In other words, *Émile* had taken laws and society as they are and had tried to see how, by education, men might be made different. The *Social Contract* sets out to take men as they are, and explores how the State could be made different. But it is not just a Utopia, a description of an ideal or 'perfect' State. It is a dis-cussion of how governments ought to be set up and run if they are to be 'good governments'. But what is a 'good government'?

This problem in 1762 – the problem of just what was meant by a 'good government' – lay at the very heart of political theory. Perhaps it always does. Thinkers of the previous two centuries, like Machiavelli or Hobbes, had accustomed people to thinking in terms of sovereignty: to the need in any State for there to be one ultimate source of authority charged to make laws and uphold good order. But other thinkers, like John Locke and Montesquieu, had been concerned lest putting so much emphasis on state sovereignty might destroy the rights and freedoms of individuals. The favourite theory of seventeenth-century Europe was the theory that kings ruled by a direct commission from God and exercised their sacred authority by 'divine right'. It made the claims of government absolute: on the other hand, the theory of the 'natural rights of man' made the claims of individual citizens absolute. Nobody had satisfactorily solved the problem of how to reconcile these two absolute claims. Clearly both could not be upheld at once, and neither seemed to fit at all well with practical experience, which was that if the absolute State led to tyranny and slavery, absolute freedom for the individual led to anarchy and collapse. Locke wanted government by consent: Rousseau wanted more than that. Here is his own statement of the dilemma which he set out to solve in the *Social Contract* –

'The problem is to find a form of association which will defend and protect with the whole common force the person and goods of each associate, and in which each, while uniting himself with all, may still obey himself alone, and remain as free as before.' This is the fundamental problem of which the *Social Contract* provides the solution . . .

If we discard from the social compact what is not of its essence, we shall find that it reduces itself to the following terms: 'Each of us puts his person and all his power in common under the supreme direction of the general will, and, in our corporate capacity, we receive each member as an indivisible part of the whole.'

At once, in place of the individual personality of each contracting party, this act of association creates a moral and collective body, composed of as many members as the assembly contains votes, and receiving from this act its unity, its common identity, its life and its will. This public person, so formed by the union of all other persons, formerly took the name of *city*, and now takes that of *Republic* or *body politic*; it is called by its members *State* when passive, *Sovereign* when active, and *Power* when compared with others like itself.

This special kind of association – a 'moral and collective body' which is created by general agreement of the whole community – has, according to Rousseau, a 'general will'; and if we look for where 'sovereignty' in the old sense is to be found in a Republic, it will be found to lie here, in the 'general will'. So the basic idea is this rather complicated but crucial one of the 'general will'. First, what is it not?

It is not, Rousseau says, just the sum total of all the separate wills of the individual members who entered into the Social Contract, even if they should happen to be unanimous about any policy or decision. Likewise, of course, it is not just a majority decision, however large the majority may be. It is fully the 'general will', in his idealized sense, only when it aims at the *common good* and when it is spontaneously supported by all citizens of *goodwill* who have at heart whatever reason and experience and their own private consciences tell them is for the common good. In other words it is a moral, qualitative idea, more like a great surge of patriotic spirit in a time of crisis. One thinks of the universal refusal of the whole people of Britain to come to terms with Hitler in 1940 after Dunkirk and during the Battle of Britain. It is a matter of the heart and of conscience, as well as of the head. Anything else is either what he calls 'partial' wills – the group-interests and sectional aims of some members of the community who belong to (say) a political party or a trade union – or else a mere sum of particular aims, which he calls the 'will of all' –

The general will, to be really such, must be general in its object as well as its essence; it must both come from all and apply to all; and it loses its natural rectitude when it is directed to some particular and determinate object, because in such a case we are judging of something foreign to us, and have no true principle of equity to guide us ... It should be seen from the foregoing that what makes the will general is less the number of voters than the common interest uniting them. ...

Rousseau regards this as very important and writes a good deal about the distinction between the 'general will', in his special new sense, and that 'will of all', which is just the sum total of all selfish, particular wills. Each citizen is capable of understanding the general good because he is himself part of the whole. But you cannot expect him to have as much sympathy with other people's sectional interests as with his own. Rousseau claims that the general will in action *is* sovereignty, and since the general will emanates from the community as a whole, so sovereignty must reside in the community as a whole. It is this that makes Rousseau a great democratic theorist. He argues that sovereignty cannot be surrendered, or delegated to any one person or group of people. It cannot be exercised at all through elected representatives, so he is not interested in proportional representation or ingenious electoral systems. He says that even the English, who alone at that time had a limited representative government, are free only during elections. His ideal State is a very small, compact State, more like the tiny City-States of the Greeks or his native Geneva, than the huge nation-states of our times. The essential is that each individual should feel personally involved. Democracy means personally taking part in political decisions. He knows that such an image of democracy is ideal, and even admits: 'Were there a people of gods, their government would be democratic. So perfect a government is not for men.' In such a democracy, however, sovereignty is indivisible, for it reflects the unity of the general will. It is also – by definition – infallible, for if things go wrong it merely means that people were mistaken in what they took to be the general will.

There is often a great deal of difference, Rousseau insists, between the will of all and the general will –

... the latter considers only the common interest, while the former takes private interest into account, and is no more than the sum of particular wills: but take away from these same wills the pluses and minuses that cancel one another, and the general will remains, as the sum of the differences.

This last remark has caused students of the *Social Contract* a good deal of puzzled conjecture and thought-reading. Either Rousseau is saying that it is possible to discover quite easily the general will from the will of all, by merely cancelling out the competing particular wills and taking what is left, which seems to mean a possible minority attitude or the margin of a majority attitude; or else he is utterly confused and unclear. I believe the second to be true, that he is simply confused, because this account of how a general will can be evolved out of the will of all simply does not fit with other things he has to say about the general will itself.

He insists, for example, that groups and associations within the State are bad because they get between the citizen and his public duty and, as it were, distract him from a clear, steady vision of the good of the whole community. They contribute only to the sum of particular wills and sectional interests. They are a positive hindrance to discovering the general will –

When factions arise, and partial associations are formed at the expense of the great association, the will of each of these associations becomes general in relation to its members, while it remains particular in relation to the State.

It is therefore essential Rousseau argues, if the general will is to find expression, that there should be –

no partial society within the State, and that each citizen should think only his own thoughts. ... But if there are partial societies, it is best to have as many as possible and to prevent them from being unequal.

This picture of a democratic State seems very far away from ours. We have come to think that one of the hallmarks of a free and democratic society is the existence of a large number of free associations and corporations of all kinds and sizes – churches, trade unions and universities, every sort of voluntary society, and above all freely formed political parties. We regard at least two big political parties as the indispensable evidence that a State is democratic – as proof that people are free to criticize and oppose and try to replace in power whichever party happens to make up the government at any moment. Does this mean that it is wrong, then, to hail Rousseau as a democratic thinker?

Some critics have said that it is. They have made a distinction between our idea of a free democratic society, with a whole mesh of overlapping associations and groups of all kinds, which they call a 'pluralist society': and Rousseau's vision of a small, tightly knit, monolithic community, which may be independent and self-governing but lacks freedom of association, and which they call 'totalitarian democracy'. Certainly Rousseau's arguments against freedom of association were used by his most fervent disciples, the Girondins and Jacobins during the French Revolution, to turn the church into a state department, to forbid unions of workers or employers, and to liquidate opposition parties during the Reign of Terror. So Rousseau's ideas seem to have in them some rather high-powered implications, hostile to freedom as we understand it.

It has been suggested that Rousseau must be seen as the theorist of the democratic *movement*, but not of the democratic *State*. He teaches that freedom and equality are indispensable to one another as ideals, that government ought to rest on the moral purpose of the whole community, and that the moral basis of politics matters more than any institutional forms. He is, *par excellence*, the philosopher of that great 'democratic revolution' which began in the eighteenth century and went on gaining sporadic victories ever since, and which only in recent years historians have come to see more clearly in one piece.* But his ideas have less meaning – certainly they are more difficult to apply – in an established democratic state of our modern kind, which rests on the very tensions between

*See R. R. Palmer, *The Age of the Democratic Revolution: The Challenge* (Princeton, Princeton University Press 1959) especially Chapter V; and for a discussion of the whole notion, Guy S. Métraux and François Crouzet, *The Nineteenth-Century World* (New York, Mentor Books, 1963) pp. 44–85.

freedom and authority which Rousseau hoped to eliminate.

Nowhere do his ideas seem to us more backward-looking or less prophetic than in his discussion of religious toleration, or the right relations between Church and State. Nearly a century after Locke, and in the age of Voltaire, he still found the idea of full religious toleration inconceivable. He therefore found political toleration equally inconceivable, in terms in which we now regard it as the prerequisite of democratic government.

His views on what he calls 'civil religion' and the limits of religious toleration recall Luther's in their narrowness rather than Locke's in their breadth. It is so important for a community that its citizens should have a religious belief that the sovereign authority has a right, he believed, to fix the articles of faith 'not exactly as religious dogmas, but as social sentiments without which a man cannot be a good citizen or a faithful subject'. Atheists will be banned as inevitably unreliable because they are 'faithless'. The State may be unable to compel men to believe the articles of faith but 'it can banish from the State whoever does not believe them'. If anyone, after publicly recognizing the required dogmas, behaves as if he does not believe them, he can be put to death for 'lying before the law'. Toleration, however, should be granted to all religions so long as they tolerate others and so long as their own dogmas contain nothing contrary to the duties of citizenship. Banishment of unbelievers, in true Lutheran style, will not be for impiety, but for being anti-social.

Rousseau's account of an imposed 'civil religion' is not unlike the situation in the one-party 'People's Democracies' of eastern Europe. It professes a distinction in theory which has little significance in practice. It matters little to a man that he is banished for being anti-social rather than for being impious, so long as he is banished. Likewise no government minds a theoretical distinction which leaves it free to act anyhow. There is something almost hypocritical, or at least ostrich-like, in maintaining that religious belief is a private matter of conscience, but that non-believers can be deprived, by a decision of the sovereign, of all their citizen rights. His community has to have some cement of a common faith, though that faith need only be what the State wants it to be.

We are still left with the question of what message Rousseau has for us today in the West, with our huge Nation-States and our complex, industrial, democratic societies. Is his idea of the general will a useful idea for us, helping us to understand better what democratic ideals and government really mean? Or is it due to be discarded as the out-of-date dream of a romantic eighteenth-century French visionary?

If it is disentangled from its eighteenth-century trimmings it still has a lot of usefulness today. We can see this if we look closer at the idea he made more explicit in *Émile* than in the *Social Contract*: his idea of 'Nature' and of 'Natural Man'. As a wayward creature, always at variance with the attitudes and conventions of his day, Rousseau was aware of how much human unhappiness came from frictions and conflicts between the individual and society. He blamed most of such unhappiness on society: if men are wicked it is because bad upbringing and environment have corrupted them. It is bad social arrangements, unjust laws, despotic governments, that cause evil. Man is by nature good. If he were not corrupted by bad conditions, his natural goodness would out and make for a free society based on equality and justice. From this starting-point he wrote both these books that came out just over two hundred years ago. *Émile* begins: 'God makes all things good; man meddles with them and they become evil.' The first chapter of the *Social Contract* begins: 'Man was born free; and everywhere he is in chains.' Rousseau rather liked such oracular and epigrammatic beginnings; but they show how much his thinking started from this one doctrine of Natural Man – Man is by Nature good, yet good does not prevail.

The idea of man's natural goodness collided, of course, with the traditional Christian doctrine of original sin and the need for redemption. Modern psychologists would cast doubt on both ideas, but many of them would agree with Rousseau's general conclusions, if not with his basic doctrine. They would say that man is 'naturally' neither good nor bad but just neutral – a complex of different impulses capable of being moulded a good deal, though not entirely, by his up-bringing, education and the total environment, both material and moral, of the community in which he lives. So, with Rousseau, they would attach a lot of importance to the effects on men of the community in which they grow up and live their lives.

It is this emphasis on conditions that entitles Rousseau to be called, as he often has been called, the father of modern socialism. The search for ways of abolishing extremes of poverty and wealth, of establishing fuller social equality and justice in place of privilege and hardship, has often been inspired by ideas that derive from Rousseau. Even our modern Welfare State, with its aim of removing what Lord Beveridge called the five giants of Want, Squalor, Ignorance, Disease and Idleness, rests on the belief that it is by attacking bad social conditions and setting up new social services that progress will come – even moral progress.

It is true that some of the more confusing remarks that Rousseau made about how absolute must be the sovereignty of the general will and about the merits of a civil religion neatly tailored to suit the convenience of the State, betrayed him into the hands of dictators and tyrannical movements. Had he encountered these he would certainly have opposed them vehemently. But it is equally true that other of his doctrines – such as the faith that man is by nature good, and the virtue of small communities – were seized upon as the basis for theories of anarchism, for discarding the claims of the State altogether. Is Rousseau, then, to be seen as at once a democrat, a socialist, a champion of totalitarian despotism and an anarchist? If so, he must indeed be a very remarkable philosopher.

Rousseau himself was certainly not all these things at once. He was the victim of great internal psychological tensions and intellectual conflicts. In one mood he was a 'child of Nature' – impulsive, wayward, self-assertive, violently in-dividualistic and almost a practising anarchist. In another, he was the stern moralist, urging a sensitive awareness of duty to serve the common good as the highest civic virtue. So his philosophy was, not unnaturally, inconsistent and at times confused. In religion he was brought up in Calvinist Geneva in a strict Puritan society, then became converted to Roman Catholicism, then abandoned it for Calvinism again, and ended in a vague cult of 'natural religion'. A man who changed so often in his faith, and incidentally in his personal affections, for he was pathologically quarrelsome and touchy, need not be expected to be calmly logical or rationally consistent in his political and social philosophy.

But if Rousseau was not all these different things at once, neither was he all of them in turn. He is liable to use turns of phrase which seem highly despotic – that man may be 'forced to be free' or that censorship is only 'the declaration of the public judgement'. But on balance he is always eventually on the side of individual freedom, fuller social justice, democracy even as we understand it, rather than of a monolithic, highly disciplined community. The uses that have been made of his political ideas by subsequent thinkers and political movements are even more variegated and contrasting than were the implications that he himself drew from them.

This in itself is often the sign of a really seminal and important thinker. Standing at the crossroads of thought at a critical historical moment – in this instance on the brink of the French Revolution, the age of Napoleon and of modern nationalism, democracy and socialism – Rousseau has been the fountainhead for many different streams of thought which have flowed on to our times, taking new and surprising forms as they proceed.

The sort of society Rousseau really wanted was probably a 'property-owning democracy' – a community in which wealth was not necessarily equally distributed, but which knew neither great wealth nor deep poverty. But in discussing economic matters he was liable to put forward ideas that sounded violently revolutionary, and which sometimes really were revolutionary. This, for example, from his *Discourse on the Origin of Inequality* of 1755 –

The first man who, having enclosed a piece of ground, bethought himself of saying 'This is mine', and found people simple enough to believe him, was the real founder of civil society. From how many crimes, wars and murders, from how many horrors and misfortunes might not any one have saved mankind, by pulling up the stakes, or filling up the ditch, and crying to his fellows, 'Beware of listening to this impostor; you are undone if you once forget that the fruits of the earth belong to us all, and the earth itself to nobody.'

Or, in his *Discourse on Political Economy* of 1758, he has this to say about the relations between rich and poor –

The terms of the social compact between these two estates of men may be summed up in a few words. 'You have need of me, because I am rich and you are poor. We will therefore come to an agreement. I will permit you to have the honour of serving me, on condition that you bestow on me the little you have left, in return for the pains I shall take to command you.'

Was Rousseau consistent? Perhaps the greatest thinkers are not strictly consistent, and would not be great if they were. But at least in the most central idea of all his political thinking – the idea of the general will as the foundation of human society and the source of sovereignty in the State – two different elements combined. There was the Rousseau who was revolutionary and romantic (let's call him Jean-Jacques), the precursor of the whole romantic movement in art and literature. There was also Rousseau the champion of a middle-class, property-owning democracy, soberly dedicated to the ideals of Liberty, Equality, Fraternity. In one the heart ruled; in the other, the head. In Jean-Jacques Rousseau's own writings, as later in the actual course of the French Revolution, the two merged to make one very explosive compound: the democratic doctrine of the Sovereignty of the People, which for the last two hundred years has dominated world history.

BOOK-LIST

The handiest editions of the relevant texts are –

ROUSSEAU, J.-J., *The Social Contract and Discourses*, translated with an introduction by G. D. H. Cole (Everyman's Library, 1913 or later edition).

ROUSSEAU, J.-J., *Émile*, translated by Barbara Foxley, introduction by A. Boutet de Monvel (Everyman's Library, 1911 or later edition).

On Rousseau's political ideas, there are lengthy extracts from his writings and a useful essay (by ROMAIN ROLLAND) in *French Thought in the Eighteenth Century: Rousseau, Voltaire, Diderot*, with an introduction by Geoffrey Brereton (London, 1953); the best single study is ALFRED COBBAN, *Rousseau and the Modern State* (London, 1934).

A classical discussion of the idea of the 'general will' by a subsequent political thinker of wide influence may be found in T. H. GREEN, *Lectures on the Principles of Political Obligation* (London, 1931 or later editions).

Though there is, among the vast amount of literature about him, no adequate biography in English, the more recent lines of interpretation of his life and significance are briefly discussed in PETER GAY, *The Party of Humanity: Studies in the French Enlightenment*, Part III (London, 1964).

See also the Book-list on Montesquieu above, p. 94.

8

TOM PAINE AND THE RIGHTS OF MAN

J. HAMPDEN JACKSON

IT is no use looking in Tom Paine's *Rights of Man* or anywhere else in his writings for a systematic exposition of political ideas. Tom Paine was not that kind of writer, nor that kind of man.

He was not an intellectual of the kind that John Locke so supremely was. He used to say that he never read any books except his own: and if that is not precisely true, it is near enough. He was never a man of the study, and the wonder is that he was ever able to put into any sort of order the bees that buzzed in his bonnet. He had no formal education beyond a few years in the grammar school of his native Thetford in Norfolk, and even there he was debarred from learning Latin because his Quaker father believed, with some justification, that the classical Latin authors were morally an unedifying lot.

For the first thirty-seven years of his life he was obscure, trying to earn his living first in his father's trade as a stay-maker, then as an Excise official of the lowest grade, then as a tobacconist in a small way, and he had every reason to think of himself as a failure when he sailed for Philadelphia in 1774 with letters of introduction from Benjamin Franklin in his pocket.

He had failed to make the grade as a stay-maker, had been dismissed from the Customs Service, had gone bankrupt as a tobacconist, but of course he was not a failure. He had seen what was wrong in England; he had formed his Radical ideas; he had learned to use his pen, and he had met and conversed with some of the sharpest wits in London.

Tom Paine arrived in New England at a time when political

ideas were being put into action. A few months after he landed, the Colonists were at war with their British rulers. His first major work, *Common Sense*, was to be a vindication of the American Revolution. In later years he was to use Common Sense as his signature, describing himself as 'a man who considers the world as his home, and the good of it in all places as his object'. It was this spirit that brought him to Paris in 1789 to live through the first glorious months of the French Revolution, and his book the *Rights of Man* was a vindication of that revolution.

It is probable that Paine did not start writing this second of his major works with Burke's ideas in mind, but the publication of Burke's *Reflections on the Revolution in France* gave him a peg to hang it on. And from the point of view of circulation it was just as well that he did, for the public dearly loves controversy, and when the first part of the *Rights of Man* was published early in 1791 it became an immediate best-seller. If we are to believe Paine, 'it had the greatest run of anything ever published in this country'. The second part, which appeared a year later, went on with the belabouring of Burke and was equally successful.

People who do not like what Paine stood for – and there are as many of them now as there were when he wrote – dismiss him as a journalist, a pamphleteer, a polemicist, a vulgarizer. Certainly he was all that, though it is hard to see why they should be terms of abuse. It is arguable that he was not an original thinker. But who, for that matter, ever was? Paine may not be the first man to conceive the idea of univer-sal suffrage, but he is recognized as the first to advocate it in America, in France and, for that matter, in England. What must be admitted is that it was thanks to Tom Paine that the ideas which we now connect with the word 'Democracy' gained popular currency in North America, in Britain, in France, and in Latin America as well. These ideas seem respect-ably ordinary, now that we have adopted so many of them. At the time when he published them they were disreputable, extraordinary, and either abominable or liberating according to the reader's way of thinking.

What gained such a vast readership for Paine's writings was not so much their controversial, disrespectful tone as the fact that they were written for ordinary men in the belief that the ordinary man could master the science of politics. That science, Paine taught, was just a matter of Common Sense. Now, nearly two hundred years after he wrote, Paine's words are still being read, not so much by academics as by ordinary men who come to them for a comfort and inspiration they can find in no other political philosopher.

In Paine's writing they can hear the man talking, a man of their own sort –

What is Government more than the management of the affairs of a Nation? It is not, and from its nature cannot be, the property of any particular man or family, but of the whole community, at whose expense it is supported; and though by force and contrivance it has been usurped into an inheritance, the usurpation cannot alter the right of things. Sovereignty, as a matter of right, appertains to the Nation only, and not to any individual; and a Nation has at all times an inherent, indefeasible right to abolish any form of Government it finds inconvenient, and to establish such as accords with its interest, disposition, and happiness. The romantic and barbarous distinction of men into Kings and subjects though it may suit the condition of courtiers, cannot that of citizens; and is exploded by the principle upon which Governments are now founded. Every citizen is a member of the sovereignty, and, as such, can acknowledge no personal subjection: and his obedience can only be to the laws.

Which laws, and what constitutes the sort of law to which obedience must be given? Paine will come back to that. But first he has something to say about hereditary systems of government. Whether by monarchies or by aristocracies, the hereditary system is equally absurd and contemptible, and that for one simple reason –

Experience, in all ages and in all countries, has demonstrated that it is impossible to control nature in her distribution of mental powers. She gives them as she pleases. Whatever is the rule by which she, apparently to us, scatters them among mankind, that rule remains a secret to man. It would be as ridiculous to attempt to fix the hereditaryship of human beauty as of wisdom. Whatever wisdom constituently is, it is like a seedless plant; it may be reared when it appears, but it cannot be voluntarily produced. There is always a sufficiency somewhere in the general mass of society for all purposes; but with respect to the parts of society, it is continually changing its place. It rises in one today, in another tomorrow, and has most probably visited in rotation every family of the earth, and again withdrawn.

As this is in the order of nature, the order of Governments must necessarily follow it, or Government will, as we see it does, degenerate into ignorance. The hereditary system, therefore, is as repugnant to human wisdom as to human rights; it is as absurd as it is unjust.

As the republic of letters brings forward the best literary productions, by giving to genius a fair and universal chance; so the representative system of Government is calculated to produce the wisest laws, by collecting wisdom from where it can be found. I smile to myself when I contemplate the ridiculous insignificance into which literature and all the sciences would sink, were they made hereditary; and I carry the same idea into Governments. An hereditary governor is as ridiculous as an hereditary author. I know not whether Homer or Euclid had sons; but I will venture an opinion if they had, and had left their works unfinished, those sons could not have completed them.

Elected government, representative of the people, was the only form of government in which Paine could see any sense. Government by direct democracy, when all citizens take part in the process of law-making, may be all very well in a very small community – it might have been all very well in ancient Athens; but even there it might be better to elect representatives, and in larger communities representatives are a necessity.

Paine may have been more confident than we are in the ability of the people to elect wise and capable representatives – there were only two remotely representative governments in all the world at the time he was writing, one in the United States, the other in France – but he was not as starry-eyed as his opponents have made him out to be. He recognized that the chosen representatives of the people might make mistakes, but in that case, he insisted, 'though there may be error, there is no injustice'. Where injustice might creep in, he saw, was through majority-rule turning to persecution of minorities. He saw no cut-and-dried way of preventing this – any more than we can today; he could only insist that the majority must not impose conditions on a minority that are different from the conditions it imposes on itself.

Like other writers in the eighteenth century, Paine saw the justification of government in a 'Social Contract', but for him it was a contract, not between governors and the governed, but between the people themselves –

It has been thought a considerable advance towards establishing the principles of Freedom to say that Government is a compact between those who govern and those who are governed; but this cannot be true, because it is putting the effect before the cause; for as man must have existed before Governments existed, there necessarily was a time when Governments did not exist, and consequently there could originally exist no governors to form such a compact with. The fact therefore must be that the *individuals themselves*, each in his own personal and sovereign right, entered into a *compact with each other* to produce a Government: and this is the only mode in which Governments had a right to arise, and the only principle in which they have a right to exist.

As Paine saw it, the only legitimate origin of government was in this compact between individuals representing the Nation. They would draw up a Constitution laying down the principles on which the government would be established, the way in which it would be organized, the powers that it would have, and so on. Only thus, and on the basis of a Constitution that could be referred to clause by clause, could a legitimate government come into being. This was more or less what was happening in France when Paine was writing. It was more or less what had happened in America while he was there and taking a constructive part in the process behind the scenes.

Also like other philosophers of the eighteenth century Paine was preoccupied with 'Natural Rights'. Most writers got their readers into a great fog about this, but Paine, with his gift of speaking to the common man, cut a straight path through the murk –

Natural rights are those which appertain to man in right of his existence. Of this kind are the intellectual rights, or rights of the mind, and also those rights of acting as an individual for his own comfort and happiness, which are not injurious to the natural rights of others. Civil rights are those which appertain to man in the right of his being a member of society. Every civil right has for its foundation some natural right pre-existing in the individual, but to the enjoyment of which his individual power is not, in all cases, sufficiently competent. Of this kind are all those which relate to security and protection.

This brings us to the famous Declaration of the Rights of Man and of Citizens. Many people who have heard of this Declaration think that its author was Tom Paine, and that he proclaimed it. In fact, of course, it was made by the National Assembly of France in 1789. In this book Paine was its translator and champion. But in reality he was rather more than that. He had talked with and had some influence on the Frenchmen who drafted the document, and he had had more talk with and doubtless more influence on the Americans who drew up the Declaration of Independence to which the French Declaration of Rights owed so much. And it is to Paine that the English-speaking world owes its acquaintance with this most seminal of all political documents.

He quotes the first four clauses of the French Declaration, in his own translation, again and again –

First: Men are born, and always continue, free and equal in respect of their rights. Civil distinctions, therefore, can be founded only on public utility.

Note that no one in his senses ever said that men are born equal in everything. They are born equal in rights. We might well ask ourselves how far that equality of rights is recognized in practice today, even in this most civilized and democratic country. And how far, even here and now, are distinctions founded only on usefulness to society?

Second: The end of all political associations is the preservation of the natural and imprescriptible rights of man. These rights are Liberty, Property, Security, and the right to resist oppression.

Paine did not need to go on to define the sort of oppression which all men have the right to resist. He did not need to say what was meant by security, though today when social security is apt to connote something to do with the Welfare State, we may have to remind ourselves that in those days it meant freedom from arbitrary arrest. He did not even attempt to define property, and comfortable readers may be relieved and surprised to find Paine and the French Revolutionaries regarding property as an inviolable and sacred right. Perhaps Paine was thinking of property as the tool of a man's trade, without which he cannot earn his living – thinking of it as the equipment necessary to a stay-maker, as the horse without which he could not have made his rounds as an Excise official.

Liberty, the first of all the rights of man, will be defined in the fourth clause of the Declaration, in less than a dozen words, leaving no room for misunderstanding though a good deal of room for disagreement. The third clause runs –

Third: The Nation is essentially the source of all sovereignty; nor can any individual, or any body of men, be entitled to any authority that is not expressly derived from it.

The Nation! Has anyone ever given a satisfying definition of that entity? At the present time it is apt to be associated with national sovereignty, and people talk about national sovereignty being on the way out. But at the time of the French Revolution and for long afterwards it was an emotive word. The Nation meant the whole society to which one belonged. It was based on a feeling of belonging together. It was the People.

And now we come to the definition of Liberty –

Fourth: Political Liberty consists in the power of doing whatever does not injure another. The exercise of the natural rights of every man has no other limits than those which are necessary to secure to every *other* man the free exercise of the same rights. And those limits are determinable only by the law.

It is a commonsense definition. Liberty consists in the power to do whatever does not injure another. Churchmen were – and are – appalled by this definition. They like to call Paine an atheist, but if they read his books they would see that the only question is whether he was a Deist or a Theist. A more usual line of attack is that Paine stressed the Rights and ignored the Duties of man. But did he? He said very definitely that –

A Declaration of Rights is, by reciprocity, a declaration of duties also. Whatever is *my* right as a man is also the right of another; and it becomes my duty to guarantee as well as to possess.

But to return to Clause Four, where it is laid down that: 'The limits of Liberty are to be determined only by law.' Everything depends, then, on what law means. Nearly half the whole Declaration is taken up with answering this question. The really significant words are these –

The law is an expression of the will of the community. All citizens have a right to concur, either personally or through their representatives, in its formation.

The principles, the bases, of political democracy are all in the Declaration of Rights – the sovereignty of the people; law made by elected representatives; the equality of all men in respect of their rights, the first of all rights being liberty, which is the power to do whatever does not injure another. They were proclaimed a hundred and seventy-five years ago, and it has taken us to this day to understand their implications and to get them enforced in a few comparatively small areas of the world.

But Paine's *Rights of Man* is concerned with economic and social as well as with strictly political ideas, and some of these need pressing today almost as much as they did in the eighteenth century. What he has to say about the need for progressive taxation is valid still in these days when non-progressive indirect taxes are being increased in proportion to progressive, direct taxes and weigh disproportionately on the poor. And what he has to say about commerce is particularly relevant to our current debates about trade with under-developed countries –

Like blood, Commerce cannot be taken from any of the parts, without being taken from the whole mass in circulation, and all partake of the loss. When the ability of any nation to buy is destroyed, it equally involves the seller. Could the Government of England destroy the commerce of all other Nations, she would most effectually ruin her own ... The ability to buy must reside out of herself; and, therefore, the prosperity of any commercial Nation is regulated by the prosperity of the rest. If they are poor she cannot be rich, and her condition, be it what it may, is an index of the height of the commercial tide in other Nations.

Here and there in the *Rights of Man* will be found what no other eighteenth-century writer made anyone hear. Paine insisted on the instruction of youth and on the public support of the aged. Our present efforts in this country to extend education and to provide adequate old-age pensions owe much to Tom Paine, who advocated –

making that provision for the instruction of youth and the support of age, as to exclude, as much as possible, profligacy from the one and despair from the other.

Paine could never understand why he was persecuted. Everything he wrote was surely the most obvious Common Sense and must be seen to be such by everybody? In fact, of course, it was dangerously inflammatory. Part One of the *Rights of Man* – the part in which he translated the French Declaration – escaped the arm of the law, but Part Two went too far. Here he called monarchy a 'silly, contemptible thing'. He inveighed against the Bill of Rights, which he called a bill of wrongs and insults. There was a clause in that Bill binding subjects to obedience for ever. But no contract can possibly bind people for ever, he insisted. It is the same insistence that the Republic of Panama has more recently been making against the claims of the United States to bind Panama in perpetuity by the 1903 Treaty.

He scoffed at the British Constitution for not being a constitution at all. It was not written down, no one could refer to it; it was nothing but an arbitrary selection of precedents, and precedent is the opposite of a rational, commonsense basis for the establishment of government in the conduct of affairs.

So Tom Paine was declared an outlaw. Before he could be seized he got out of the country to France, where he had been elected a member of the Convention. Soon even revolutionary France got too hot for him, and he found himself in prison in the Luxembourg, where he nearly died. He spent his declining years in the United States and was never properly rehabilitated in this country.

Where he belongs is not territorially in England, or France, or even in the United States but in all three countries and in any others where the yeast of the democratic movement is working. In England he belongs with Jeremy Bentham (1748–1832) with whom he shared the honour of receiving French citizenship at the hands of the Legislative Assembly; his most direct successor was William Cobbett (1763–1835), and his genes are to be found in most of the nineteenth-century Radicals. In continental Europe his place is with the Enlightenment. He was often misunderstood – Madame de Staël called him a metaphysician and said that he had 'written a book in order to raise demagoguery into dogma' – but he is central to the whole eighteenth-century tradition of Rationalism. In America, where he began as the *protégé* of Benjamin Franklin, and went on to become a friend of Thomas Jefferson, he lives on as a protagonist of democracy and also as a prophet in the sense that Walt Whitman is a prophet –

O ye that love mankind: ye that dare oppose, not only the tyranny stand forth: every spot of the old world is overrun with oppression. Freedom hath been hunted round the globe. Asia and Africa have long expelled her – Europe regards her like a stranger, and England hath given her warning to depart. O! receive the fugitive, and prepare in time an asylum for mankind.

The scene to fix Tom Paine in our memory as the central figure in the international democratic movement took place in 1789, when Lafayette handed him the key of the Bastille to take to George Washington.

BOOK-LIST

The *Rights of Man* is most easily available in Dent's Everyman's Library. The most recent book on Paine is A. O. ALDRIDGE, *Man of Reason* (London, 1960). W. E. WOODWARD, *Tom Paine: America's Godfather* (London, 1946) is also worth reading though less reliable. Of the earlier biographies the best is M. D. CONWAY, *The Life of Thomas Paine*, 2 vols. (New York, 1892). *See also* the more general works listed for Montesquieu and Rousseau (above) and Burke (below); and MAX BELOFF (editor), *The Debate on the American Revolution, 1761–1783* (London, 1949).

9

BURKE AND THE CONSERVATIVE TRADITION

C. W. PARKIN

THERE is a saying of Burke as a very young man which epitomizes both his career and his philosophy. 'Man is made for speculation and action,' he said, 'and when he pursues his nature he succeeds best in both.'* Unlike many of the thinkers discussed in this book, Burke was, for a great part of his life, a professional politician. Hardly any of his political writings are the production of the armchair student. They are speeches and tracts called forth by, and addressed to, some issue in the political world of the day. And this is true of the pamphlet for which he is most famous, his *Reflections on the Revolution in France*. As the very title indicates, he is not offering an abstract, formal treatise of political philosophy such as Rousseau's *Social Contract*, but a commentary on certain contemporary happenings. What in fact we find is (in form) a letter, addressed to 'a very young gentleman at Paris', and (in content) an unsystematic, turbulent discussion of the events, personalities and theories of the early months of the French Revolution. This type of engaged thought, this union of speculation and action, so characteristic of Burke, is both attractive and challenging: attractive, because of its immediacy, its call on our united resources of intelligence, imagination and feeling; challenging, because it is left to us to extract from this living experience its enduring ideas and its continuing suggestiveness.

The French Revolution began in May 1789 in State bankruptcy, and the summoning, for the first time since 1614, of the States-General. Within that antique body a struggle for

*H. V. F. Somerset (ed.), *A Note-book of Edmund Burke*, p. 87.

power at once ensued between the privileged orders and the Commons, from which the Commons, representatives of the middle class, emerged victorious. Then the newly named National Assembly embarked on a course of fundamental political reconstruction: the electrifying Declaration of the 'Rights of Man'; the abolition of feudal privilege; and far-ranging constitutional debates and transformations. This fevered, tempestuous political activity, continuing over many months, was punctuated by certain days of unique drama. One was 14 July 1789, the day on which the people of Paris attacked and stormed the royal fortress, the Bastille, symbol of old despotism. Another was 6 October 1789, when the Parisian crowd escorted the royal family, as virtual prisoners, from the great palace at Versailles back into residence in the capital. Much was still to come, which would eclipse even these stupendous events; but such were the developments in France which were before Burke's eyes in the composition of his *Reflections*. He was working on the manuscript throughout 1790, revising, enlarging; and it was published on 1 November of that year. Its impact was instantaneous and immense. Burke's friend Windham wrote –

Never was there, I suppose, a work so valuable in its kind, or that displayed powers of so extraordinary a nature. It is a work that may seem capable of overturning the National Assembly, and turning the stream of opinion throughout Europe.

Many currents had flowed together to generate the Revolution in France. There were gross anomalies, serious injustices, deeply entrenched divisions; there was a general social stale-mate, before which the so-called absolute monarchy was impotent. But there was something else. The Revolution was also the culmination of a great movement of religious and ethical feeling, by no means confined to France; what historians call, and what indeed its own protagonists called, the Enlightenment. The goal, the vision, of this movement was a new stature for man. Its struggle, waged on all fronts of know-ledge and practical life, was for human self-determination; emancipation through reason from what were judged to be the degrading oppressions of traditional religion, ethics and social life, in order that man might enter into a perfection of nature as yet unattained, might be master of his historical destiny, might embark on a new epoch of secular felicity. This vision, held with all the intensity and faith of a religion, contained inevitably the most radical and subversive implications for the established order of things, for all the traditions and values by which Europe had hitherto held its course. It was pregnant with destructive, as well as creative, power. The ferment meets us everywhere, and in many forms, in the later eighteenth century – in Rousseau's hot fusion of moral and political idealism, for example, or in the strong, naïve democratic faith of Tom Paine. It injected into the early stages of the French Revolution a hope, a sense of new human horizons, which is difficult now to conceive. We can feel a little of it in the rhapsodies of English admirers like Wordsworth –

> Bliss was it in that dawn to be alive,
> But to be young was very heaven!*

or of the politician Charles James Fox.

One of these English tributes was momentous, because it provoked Burke's *Reflections*. The Dissenting minister Richard Price preached a sermon, which not merely welcomed the Revolution in France as the glorious dawn of liberty in that land, but associated it with the English Revolution of 1688, and urged Englishmen, under its example, to press forward with reform in their own country –

What an eventful period is this! I am thankful that I have lived to it; and I could almost say, *Lord, now lettest thou thy servant depart in peace, for mine eyes have seen thy salvation* ... I have lived to see the rights of men better understood than ever; and nations panting for liberty, which seemed to have lost the idea of it ... Be encouraged, all ye friends of freedom, and writers in its defence! The times are auspicious. Your labours have not been in vain.†

* 'French Revolution, as it appeared to enthusiasts at its commencement' in *Poetical Works of Wordsworth* (Oxford Standard Authors), p. 208.
† 'A Discourse on the Love of our Country', in A. C. Ward (ed.), *A Miscellany of Tracts and Pamphlets* (World's Classics), p. 476.

Now Burke had been, almost from the beginning, alienated from this general ferment of hope. He was not unaware of the problems confronting France; but it was the destructive potentialities of the new movement which rose most vividly in his mind; for France, for all Europe, but above all for England. Price's sermon was a provocation which could not go unanswered.

His disagreement with Price was complete. To Burke the Revolution in France appeared a phenomenon of a totally new kind. It was not, like the English Revolution of 1688, a cautious, limited dynastic and constitutional change. It was a revolution based on a theory, the theory of the Rights of Man, with simple, universal, dogmatic propositions and demands. Its appeal was to the clear, unambiguous, self-justifying canons of reason, and in the name of reason it was proposing to set aside the traditions and social usages of centuries, to remodel society on an intelligible, rationally justifiable plan –

They have 'the rights of men'. Against these there can be no prescription; against these no agreement is binding: these admit no temperament, and no compromise: any thing withheld from their full demand is so much of fraud and injustice. Against these their rights of men let no government look for security in the length of its continuance, or in the justice and lenity of its administration. The objections of these speculatists, if its forms do not quadrate with their theories, are as valid against such an old and beneficent government as against the most violent tyranny, or the greenest usurpation.

But in Burke's eyes such a militant rationalism is wholly out of place in politics. The world of man is altogether too complex, too devious, too inscrutable, in its workings to be susceptible of easy rational comprehension, still less of confident interference or wholesale alteration. Social life is kept going not only by men's rational activity, but by feeling, habit, emotional attachments, conventions and traditions, without which it would collapse, yet which the eye of reason may often be powerless to penetrate. An impatient, aggressive rationalism, turned on the social order, can therefore only be subversive, as dissolvent of good institutions as of bad.

'What', Burke asks, 'would become of the world if the practice of all moral duties, and the foundations of society, rested upon having their reasons made clear and demonstrative to every individual?'* This rationalist temper, the offspring of the Enlightenment, is Burke's chief target in the *Reflections*: 'extravagant and presumptuous speculation', he calls it, 'political metaphysics'. Nevertheless, he is not answering the rationalism of the Revolution by an assertion of the irrationality of man and the world. Burke is insisting on the limitations of reason in the face of the complexity of things. If men realistically acknowledge the feebleness of human reason, and proceed with a due respect for what their predecessors have created and lived by, they can, he believes, be effective partners in their social destiny. But to assume that the truth has just come to light with oneself, after centuries of darkness, seems to Burke suicidal egotism. It is throwing away one's compass in mid-ocean.

Moreover, in another way, a rationalism of this kind seems to Burke fatally unbalanced and incomplete. The inarticulate life of society, its customary, unthinking pattern of behaviour, not only must be admitted to be a great part of social existence; Burke insists that it is, in its own way, rational too. A man's instincts and feelings may sometimes guide him to his right end when his reason misleads or fails him. Likewise, widely shared, slowly evolved, tested traditions of behaviour represent a type of wisdom, which is available to everyone, and which may serve society better in its dilemmas and crises than elaborate intellection. And in addition such feelings provide the emotional accompaniment of sound judgement, which is essential to the steadiness and consistency of behaviour. Burke calls these feelings *prejudices*; rather startlingly according to our rationalistic, and therefore disparaging, use of the word, but he is proclaiming the positive value of such unexamined convictions –

You see, Sir, that in this enlightened age I am bold enough to confess, that we are generally men of untaught feelings; that

*Preface to 'A Vindication of National Society', in *The Works of Burke* (World's Classics), Vol. I, p. 6.

instead of casting away all our old prejudices, we cherish them to a very considerable degree, and, to take more shame to ourselves, we cherish them because they are prejudices; and the longer they have lasted, and the more generally they have prevailed, the more we cherish them. We are afraid to put men to live and trade each on his own private stock of reason; because we suspect that this stock in each man is small, and that the individuals would do better to avail themselves of the general bank and capital of nations, and of ages. Many of our men of speculation, instead of exploding general prejudices, employ their sagacity to discover the latent wisdom which prevails in them. If they find what they seek (and they seldom fail), they think it more wise to continue the prejudice, with the reason involved, than to cast away the coat of prejudice, and to leave nothing but the naked reason; because prejudice, with its reason, has a motive to give action to that reason, and an affection which will give it permanence. Prejudice is of ready application in the emergency; it previously engages the mind in a steady course of wisdom and virtue, and does not leave the man hesitating in the moment of decision, sceptical, puzzled, and unresolved. Prejudice renders a man's virtue his habit; and not a series of unconnected acts. Through just prejudice, his duty becomes a part of his nature.

We do wrong, therefore, to conceive society as a mechanical assemblage of units, susceptible to arbitrary alteration by its members. It is more like an organism whose parts are deeply formed by their common life, with a tempo of change and a cumulative growth of its own. It is a living thing which reaches out into past and future. Hence a readiness to destroy, or experiment with, the social fabric saps the whole vigour of social life. It impedes the formation of habit and expectation and confidence, the creation of stable values, educational principles, social skills, by which the life of the individual is enriched, and civilization is painfully built up. Violent discontinuity, hectic change, strip the individual of his social existence; he cannot inherit, or create, or share, or transmit, anything enduring. Lost in such a void men will become, in Burke's expression, 'flies of a summer', society will dissolve into 'the dust and powder of individuality'. By contrast, the principle of the British constitution, Burke claims, has been its attachment to this ideal of continuity, the nexus of inheritance – preservation – transmission, which is nature's working in all its forms, and which secures thereby in the life of the community something of the flexibility and imperceptible growth of a natural organism –

This policy appears to me to be the result of profound reflection; or rather the happy effect of following nature, which is wisdom without reflection, and above it ... By a constitutional policy, working after the pattern of nature, we receive, we hold, we transmit our government and our privileges, in the same manner in which we enjoy and transmit our property and our lives ... Our political system is placed in a just correspondence and symmetry with the order of the world, and with the mode of existence decreed to a permanent body composed of transitory parts; wherein, by the disposition of a stupendous wisdom, moulding together the great mysterious incorporation of the human race, the whole, at one time, is never old, or middle-aged, or young, but, in a condition of unchangeable constancy, moves on through the varied tenor of perpetual decay, fall, renovation, and progression. Thus, by preserving the method of nature in the conduct of the state, in what we improve, we are never wholly new; in what we retain we are never wholly obsolete.

The historical continuity of the community therefore enforces perpetual change. At all times society is presented with anomalies, abuses, tensions, dangers, and also with new fruitful potentialities of progress, all of which may be the proper occasion for political action. What Burke insists is that political action must not be embarked on in a spirit of free invention and experiment, but as the culture of the inner growth of society. The appropriate image is that of the gardener, not of the engineer. Burke above all disputes the utopianism of the Revolution, its fanatical pursuit of social regeneration. A perfectionism of this sort, in any aspect of human affairs, opens up an unbridgeable gulf between what is and what ought to be. Not content with empirical progress, it demands a totally new order of felicity. But, Burke thinks, moral goods and evils, social advantages and inconveniences, can seldom be clear and sharp, black and white; and, even at their best, social ends must be qualified and compromised.

There is a real well-being of society, but it resides in many things, and one end ought not to be pursued to the detriment of others. Liberty, the glorious Revolutionary ideal, is a good; but so are other things, like justice, order, and peace; they are even indispensable to the reality of liberty itself. Above all, social progress lies in an extension of values already embodied in the life of society, rather than in some distant goal whose realization demands the suspension or hazard of things which are actually enjoyed; not in the sacrifice of the real present for the hypothetical future. The aim cannot be some absolute or final perfection of society, but the greatest *practicable* perfection; and this requires not only a zeal for reform, but a sense of the possible. Part of this self-limitation must be a realistic awareness of what political action can hope to accomplish, and what can only be achieved (if at all) by the unforced growth of social responsibility. And the pace of society's life must be respected, if continuity and control are to be preserved, and a durable advance secured –

If circumspection and caution are a part of wisdom, when we work only upon inanimate matter, surely they become a part of duty too, when the subject of our demolition and construction is not brick and timber, but sentient beings, by the sudden alteration of whose state, condition, and habits, multitudes may be rendered miserable ... Political arrangement, as it is a work for social ends, is to be only wrought by social means. There mind must conspire with mind. Time is required to produce that union of minds which alone can produce all the good we aim at. Our patience will achieve more than our force ... By a slow but well-sustained progress, the effect of each step is watched; the good or ill success of the first gives light to us in the second; and so, from light to light, we are conducted with safety through the whole series. We see that the parts of the system do not clash. The evils latent in the most promising contrivances are provided for as they arise. One advantage is as little as possible sacrificed to another. We compensate, we reconcile, we balance. We are enabled to unite into a consistent whole the various anomalies and contending principles that are found in the minds and affairs of men. From hence arises, not an excellence in simplicity, but one far superior, an excellence in composition.

Of course, this is a counsel of perfection. The politician cannot always choose his problems, or ends, or pace. He may often be at the mercy of events. Revolution itself may sometimes be the only recourse, as Burke allows. But he is presenting a norm of fruitful, durable change.

If this is Conservatism, it is not the conservatism of fear, of pessimism, of original sin. Burke, as much as the Revolutionaries, has an exalted notion of the ends of society and the State: 'He who gave our nature to be perfected by our virtue, willed also the necessary means of its perfection. He willed therefore the State.' That perfection, for Burke, is the integrity, the wholeness, of man's nature, the harmonious development of his powers. Burke puts it in one of his earliest writings: 'It is true indeed that enthusiasm often misleads us. So does reason too. Such is the condition of our nature; and we can't help it. But I believe that we act most when we act with all the powers of our soul.'* And Burke, as much as the Revolutionaries, in his own way, believes that the world is a unity, that society, for all its complexity, its heights and depths, forms part of a harmony of nature –

Society is indeed a contract ... it is not a partnership in things subservient only to the gross animal existence of a temporary and perishable nature. It is a partnership in all science; a partnership in all art; a partnership in every virtue, and in all perfection. As the ends of such a partnership cannot be obtained in many generations, it becomes a partnership not only between those who are living, but between those who are living, those who are dead, and those who are to be born. Each contract of each particular state is but a clause in the great primeval contract of eternal society, linking the lower with the higher natures, connecting the visible and invisible world, according to a fixed compact sanctioned by the inviolable oath which holds all physical and all moral natures, each in their appointed place.

Characteristically, Burke did not present his political principles in his own name; he offered them as no more than a

*Somerset, op. cit., p. 68.

faithful description of the traditional principles of British political life. Historically, his claim has proved to be justified. At least, in the century and a half which has followed his death, the spirit of Burke's philosophy seems to have prevailed in English public life. To the strong current of social change which began to flow, the community responded with precisely that passion for continuity which Burke had identified. In the movement towards democracy, the formal continuity of institutions was carefully preserved, while the reality was repeatedly transformed. As far as possible, new departures were grafted on to the old, the principles of the old adapted to absorb the new. This was as true of working-class developments, the Trade Union movement for example, as of the most ancient institutions of the nation. The mood of politics remained empirical rather than doctrinaire; reform and progress were still sought by culture rather than by engineering. The process had the flexibility, and the bewildering lack of definition, of animal growth. That document, the constitution, which Tom Paine demanded to be shown, was never produced. The community was content to operate political affairs within an elaborate framework of convention and moral agreement, for the most part unformulated, but deeply felt and respected. And not only the continuity, but the unity, of the social organism was preserved after the fashion Burke had tried to defend. A general moral consensus kept down the temperature of political life and moderated political partisanship. Englishmen remained solicitous to compensate, to reconcile, to balance. The social revolution was effected, not in conflict and violent displacement, but rather by the progressive extension and sympathetic reinterpretation of the original aristocratic tradition. Parties became in time nationwide, but they continued to operate within an accepted framework of national unity, to seek a nationally acceptable pace of change.

Of this tradition, this mode of political behaviour, Burke was, I think, the original and authoritative exponent. We belittle his importance if we regard him as the philosopher of one political party. As a living politician has written: 'Burke is not the philosopher of British conservatism, but of British political life from Right to Left. His spirit informs the progressive movement as much as it informs the Conservative party.' It is R. H. S. Crossman who says it.*

Nor does even this set the bounds of Burke's influence. His social ideals were repeatedly reaffirmed by some of the best minds of the nineteenth century, contemplating the spiritual and social havoc of the age. To the harsh, prosaic, mechanistic image of social union drawn by utilitarianism, the spirit of Burke opposed the organic society, mysteriously nourished by its alliance with time, its members united in a profound, richly diverse common life. In place of the materialism and stunted human ideals of industrial society, he presented the State as the trustee of civilization, society as the partnership in all perfection.

In the era of worldwide Marxism, Burke's polemic against the revolutionary idea – the utopianism, the canonization of dualism and conflict, the search for some final political solution – has not lost its relevance or cogency. And for Britain's needs, cultural as much as political, the fruitfulness of his position has not been exhausted.

The core of its continuing value lies, perhaps, in his vision of a human norm, his ideal of a unity and harmony of man's powers. That ideal has emerged in many forms: in the union of speculation and action, the marriage of intellect and feeling, of prose and passion, which Burke exemplifies in his life, his cast of mind, and his very literary style; in his ethical faith that whatever man acts out of his whole nature is right; and in his political faith that when the community respects the totality of man's powers, past and present, it achieves a real perfection and unity. This vision, by its centrality, still has something to offer, perhaps; not only against the politics of ideology and revolution, but against the politics of manipulation and mere efficiency, of self-interest, of power, of despair. In a present of staggering uncertainty, it proclaims the reality of past and future, and the assurance of continuity and direction which

* R. H. S. Crossman, 'British Political Thought in the European Tradition', in J. P. Mayer, *Political Thought: the European Tradition*, p. 188.

that can give. In a time when the human image seems to grow dim, it affirms a specific human excellence, it insists on the human scale, the human tempo, of things, it suggests a meaningful place of man in the world.

Is this 'Conservatism'? Conservatism is one of those words that demands a converse – Liberalism or Radicalism or Socialism or Revolution. But Burke's *Reflections on the Revolution in France* has more than a mere polemic importance. It would be better, indeed, if we could detach Burke's ideas from the controversy in which they were born, could break the association of his name with the Conservative tradition, and could see his position for what it is, a complete, balanced system, of politics, of morality, of man, in its own right.

BOOK-LIST

COBBAN, ALFRED (ed.), *The Debate on the French Revolution, 1789–1800* (London, 1950).

CROSSMAN, R. H. S., 'British Political Thought in the European Tradition', in J. P. Mayer, *Political Thought: the European Tradition* (London, 1942).

GRIERSON, H. J. C., 'Edmund Burke', in *The Cambridge History of English Literature*, Vol. XI, Chapter 1 (Cambridge, 1932).

PARKIN, CHARLES, *The Moral Basis of Burke's Political Thought* (Cambridge, 1956).

TALMON, J. L., *The Origins of Totalitarian Democracy* (London, 1952; Mercury Books, 1961).

WILLIAMS, RAYMOND, *Culture and Society, 1780–1950* (London, 1958; Penguin Books, 1961).

10

HEGEL AND THE NATION-STATE

R. S. PETERS

G. W. F. HEGEL was born in 1770 at Stuttgart, a typical civil servant's son. To a certain extent Hegel's way of doing philosophy was the product of his cultural heritage. He came of Swabian stock – a people in whom the easy-going expansiveness of southern Germany was mingled with the rigid rationalism of the Protestant north, especially of the Prussians. He showed no early aptitude for philosophy; his interest was more directed towards religion and history. But gradually he began to feel the attraction of Greece – its art first, and later the ideals of the city-state. His youthful enthusiasm was awakened by the French Revolution and by Rousseau, the mouthpiece of its ideals. In Rousseau, it seems, Hegel found a response to the two dominant demands of his spirit – the one for self-determination, the ideal of Luther, of Kant, of Voltaire and the Enlightenment (as the general movement away from mysticism was called), the other for participation in the organic life of a community, the ideal of the Greek city-state. The struggle to reconcile these two demands absorbed his leisure time when he was a private tutor after leaving the University of Tübingen and – together with a legacy of £300 – inspired him in 1801 to join Schelling at Jena as a champion of the so-called 'philosophy of identity'.

His career as a professional philosopher then started, though it was interrupted by Napoleon, 'that world-soul', as Hegel described him. After sundry appointments he was made professor of philosophy at Heidelberg in 1816, and in 1818 came his celebrated call to Berlin to be professor of philosophy under Frederick William III, who was in process of purging his government of liberals and reformers. He remained in Berlin till his death in 1831, the acknowledged dictator of one of the most powerful philosophical schools in the history of thought.

In the history of philosophy Hegel comes after Kant and his thought has partly to be explained as a reaction to it. There are many who regard Kant's philosophy as a magnificent synthesis of a dialectical debate; for his system welded together the contributions of British Empiricism (thinkers like Locke and Hume, with their stress on reason and experience) and Continental Rationalism. To such admirers Kant represents the crown of the Enlightenment – the belief in Reason, in toleration, and in the freedom of the individual. Kant was much impressed by the ideals of the French Revolution and was honoured as a defender of the liberal conception of the State and as a champion of a league of nations to maintain perpetual peace on earth. To such admirers of Kant, then, Hegel with his metaphysical vapourings, his worship of the State, and his idealization of war, represents the arch-priest of Romanticism who presided over the decline of German philosophy. Schopenhauer, who knew Hegel well and who respected Kant without following him, spoke for many when he said –

Hegel, installed from above, by the powers that be, as the certified Great Philosopher, was a flat-headed, insipid, nauseating, illiterate charlatan, who reached the pinnacle of audacity in scribbling together and dishing up the craziest mystifying nonsense. This nonsense has been noisily proclaimed as immortal wisdom by mercenary followers and readily accepted as such by all fools, who thus joined into as perfect a chorus of admiration as had ever been heard before. The extensive field of spiritual influence with which Hegel was furnished by those in power has enabled him to achieve the intellectual corruption of a whole generation.

This is an understandable but rather too extreme reaction to Hegel; for he did much to systematize important ideas which were then current, which were scattered through the works of Burke and Rousseau as well as in the writings of the German philosophers Herder and Lessing. The importance of tradition and customary pieties, the social roots of religion, the mystic bonds of hearth, home, and community, the massiveness of collective institutional pressures – it was to these aspects of life, whose potency was too often neglected by the more rationalistic individualistic thinkers of the Enlightenment, that Hegel gave prominence. Hegel's thinking was also much influenced by the rise of historical studies in the nineteenth century and by the intellectual ferment that developed round the idea of evolution. He is, therefore, a fascinating though an infuriating philosopher to study, because he often has a good idea which he puffs up so much that it becomes a kind of metaphysical monstrosity. Unfortunately, too, it was the expanded versions of his ideas, rather than their solid centres that, historically speaking, exerted the most influence. Consider, first of all, what he said about 'freedom' in his *Philosophy of Right* –

The state is the actuality of concrete freedom. But concrete freedom consists in this: that personal individuality and its particular interests not only achieve their complete development and gain explicit recognition for their right ... but, for one thing, they also pass over of their own accord into the interest of the universal, and for another thing, they know and will the universal. They even recognize it as their own substantive mind; they take it as their end and aim and are active in its pursuit. ... The principle of modern states has prodigious strength and depth because it allows the principle of subjectivity to progress to its culmination in the extreme of self-subsistent personal particularity and yet, at the same time, brings it back to the substantive unity and so maintains this unity in the principle of subjectivity itself.

This extract, in spite of its horrific jargon, contains an important – if unoriginal – idea, but an idea that is carried too far. Hegel saw that many liberal thinkers had pushed their conception of individual interests and personal freedom to absurd extremes. Such ideals and interests are social in character and can be achieved only within a social framework. A man, for instance, who believes in freedom of speech, is putting forward proposals which involve the permitting of public assemblies, uncensored newspapers and broadcasting. The law of the State is not necessarily an enemy of freedom: indeed without legal protection as such, a personal freedom would be an impracticable ideal, as John Locke stressed long before. But Hegel confused the *meaning* of personal freedom and personal ideals with their necessary conditions. He assumed that because *without a State* such ideals are unrealizable, they are *identical with* the interests and ideals of the State.

Hegel realized better than most that many of the individual's rights and duties, interests and claims, are bound up with his membership of lesser associations like the family which comprised what he called Civil Society. Indeed he held that without such associations people would be a formless mass. Civil society formed a sort of bridge between the individual and the State. Nevertheless he claimed that these duties – to one's family or business, profession or local community – were caught up in the supreme duty to the State. As he put it –

In contrast with the spheres of private rights and private welfare (the family and civil society) the state is from one point of view an external necessity and their higher authority; its nature is such that their laws and interests are subordinate to it and dependent on it. On the other hand, however, it is the end immanent within them, and its strength lies in the unity of its own universal end and aim with the particular interest of individuals, in the fact that individuals have duties to the state in proportion as they have rights against it.

This is the point at which Hegel pushed his good idea too far. His exaltation of the State meant, for instance, that divorce should be forbidden because the contract of marriage was largely a way of undertaking civil duties like the rearing of fresh citizens. His 'philosophy of identity' put the stamp of philosophical respectability on doctrines which are necessary for the emergence of a totalitarian State – namely, that the judgement of the individual is, as Hegel said, mere caprice, in comparison with that of the State of which he is an insignificant part; that the State provides the sole standard of morality and its laws are necessarily just; and that, because the State provides the sole standard of right, there can be no morality between States. Indeed Hegel went further. He held that war between States was necessary to their health –

War is the state of affairs which deals in earnest with the vanity of temporal goods and concerns ... This is what makes it the moment in which the ideality of the particular attains its right and is actualized. War has the higher significance that by its agency ... the ethical health of peoples is preserved in their indifference to the stabilization of finite institutions; just as the blowing of the winds preserves the sea from the foulness which would be the result of a prolonged calm, so also corruption in nations would be the product of prolonged, let alone 'perpetual' peace. The ideality which is in evidence in war ... is the same as the ideality in accordance with which the domestic powers of the State are organic moments in a whole. This fact appears in history in various forms – e.g. successful wars have checked domestic unrest and consolidated the power of the State at home. ...

Hegel's view about 'freedom' and his exaltation of the State had far-reaching repercussions. He had followers in England – Bernard Bosanquet and F. H. Bradley – who during the hey-day of British Imperialism at the turn of the century proclaimed that the individual's 'real' freedom consisted in service to the State and that his moral life was a matter of his 'station and its duties' as a citizen. Bradley looked on individual judgement as 'sheer self-conceit', and there was a tradition of public service and social conformity which emanated from Oxford University and the public schools which owed a good deal to Hegel's teaching. At its best it instilled a sense of public duty into those who governed England and who administered the British Empire; at its worst it issued in a revolting priggishness, and contempt for 'the cad' who did not conform, a belief in the maxim 'my country right or wrong' and a derisive attitude to any 'foreigner' who was not blessed with the boon of British citizenship. But the British followers of Hegel never went to his extremes in glorifying the State and the monarchy. After all, Englishmen had fought their Civil War against absolutism in the seventeenth century and, ever since, had tended to look on the State as a necessary nuisance. Their philosophical tradition, too, was too down-to-earth and tough-minded to put up for long with the gaseous balloons of Hegel's metaphysics.

But in Germany and Italy, where highly centralized nation-states were just emerging under the guidance of Bismarck and Garibaldi, Hegel's high-sounding rigmarole fell upon more receptive ears. Had he not been installed by Frederick William the Third as the state philosopher? And his doctrines have exerted an unceasing influence on German thinkers ever since. Those Germans, for instance, who later stood indicted for war-crimes like the killing of the innocent in cold blood, and who pleaded that their sole duty was to obey the orders of their superior officer, were given a good philosophical excuse by Hegel. They were putting into practice Hegel's view that –

In civilized nations true bravery consists in the readiness to give oneself wholly to the service of the State so that the individual counts but as one amongst many. No personal valour is significant; the important aspect lies in self-subordination to the universal.

The Nazis committed crimes against humanity in the name of the State; they ruthlessly broke their treaties with other nations and were equally ruthless in dealing with their own non-conformists at home. Hegel's doctrine of 'freedom' and his claim that there can be no morality between States gave them some semblance of a philosophical backing.

Hegel's fascination for 'freedom' (or rather, his peculiar concept of it) knew no bounds. For, in his view, this 'freedom', which consisted in the identification of the individual with the standards of the State and in obedience to its laws, was the latest phase in the development of a world-spirit, whose very essence was freedom –

Further, world history is not the verdict of mere might, i.e. the abstract and non-rational inevitability of a blind destiny. On the contrary, since mind is implicitly and actually reason, and reason is explicit to itself in mind as knowledge, world history is the necessary development, out of the concept of mind's freedom alone, of the moments of reason and so of the self-consciousness and freedom of mind. This development is the interpretation and actualization of the universal mind.

This grandiose conception was also suggested to him by his study of Greek thought; for Plato had made much of dialectic – a method of searching for an essence by putting forward a thesis like 'justice consists in giving every man his due' and then looking round for a case that contradicts it – for instance, where one would not return a knife to a man, which was his due as he had lent it, because he would commit murder with it. The attempt is then made to find a synthesis – a new account of justice which both includes what is acceptable in the original thesis and takes account of the objection raised.

Now this notion of dialectical progression may well be a good account of critical thought, as for instance in science or philosophy. But such thinking only exists under special conditions: in a society, that is, which encourages criticism and argument. But Hegel pictured this type of development as typical of all thought, and he also went so far as to picture history as the manifestation of such a progression on a grand scale. Things are not what they appear to be to the un-philosophical observer; the world which we see and touch is but an appearance of a process of ideas or essences working themselves out in this dialectical fashion. 'The real is the rational.' The realities beneath the appearances were the developing essences disclosed by his dialectical logic.

Hegel's fascination for dialectic seems to be another case of a fruitful idea pushed too far. It is a very illuminating descrip-tion, for instance, of the development of schools of thought or traditions of art. But Hegel did not confine his notion of dialectical developments simply to such intellectual move-ments. He thought of ideals like that of freedom as develop-ing dialectically in history. As Hegel himself put it –

The history of the world is the discipline of the uncontrolled natural will, bringing it into obedience to a universal principle and conferring subjective freedom. The East knew, and to the present day knows, only that *One* is free; the Greek and Roman world, that *Some* are free; the German world knows that *All* are free.

Again, in his conception of history as the development of spirit, Hegel had another stimulating idea which he pushed to inordinate extremes. Mind, he claimed, arises from a Nature which is quite alien and other in the sense that the imprint of mind has not been placed upon it. The development of history is the development of the impress of mind on Nature in the form of institutions and traditions by means of which we shape the external world in the satisfaction of our wants, needs, and aspirations. Gradually our external environment, like a town, bears everywhere the stamp of mentality upon it. Hegel, like Arnold Toynbee in our own time, saw civilizations arising as responses to the challenges set by the otherness of Nature – the sea, the mountains, the snow. And, as it develops, mind becomes more and more self-conscious in the achievements of what Hegel called the Absolute Spirit – Art, Religion, and Philosophy. Hegel saw what so many individualistic thinkers had missed in their accounts of the state of nature, that what we call mind or spirit needs a social context in which to exhibit itself. It is objectively manifest in developing traditions and institutions; it is not something locked up in a man's head, or a private screen on which sense-data and images from the world outside are reflected. What we call reason, for instance, is exhibited in the traditions of the Royal Society or of the Common Law Courts, and in all institutions which, as Burke also saw, fit together in a peculiarly intimate way.

Unfortunately, however, Hegel gave these very suggestive ideas a nationalistic twist that is not a necessary consequence of them. For he regarded the State as the means by which something else emerges, which is more or less the amalgam of the various traditions of art, religion, and culture, in which mind exhibited itself; this was 'the nation' – and Hegel had this to say about it –

History is mind clothing itself with the form of events or the immediate actuality of nature. The stages of its development are therefore presented as immediate natural principles. These, because they are natural, are a plurality external to one another, and they are present therefore in such a way that each of them is assigned to one nation in the external form of its geographical and anthropological conditions.

The nation to which is ascribed a moment of the Idea in the form of a natural principle is entrusted with giving complete effect to it in the advance of the self-developing self-consciousness of the world mind. This nation is dominant in world history during this one epoch, and it is only once that it can make its hour strike. In contrast with this its absolute right of being the vehicle of this present stage in the world mind's development, the minds of the other nations are without rights, and they, along with those whose hour has struck already, count no longer in world history.

The concept of 'the nation' is one of the most influential yet one of the most obscure notions in the history of political thought. For what is a 'nation' as distinct from a people living under the laws of a particular State? Does a common religion make a nation? Surely not; for the Africans are not united in this respect. Does a common language? Surely not; for the Indians and Slavs speak many languages. Does a common history? Surely not; for the Arabs, Americans, and Jews have a very variegated history. When it is said, therefore, that the State should be based on the principle of 'national self-determination', what can be meant?

Perhaps the modern belief in something called a nation, which is one of the most powerful ideas of the modern world, springs from the need to belong to a group or a tribe, to share a common life with others who may be oppressed or in danger. This need is often satisfied in a common religion. At the time when Hegel was writing, though, religion was on the decline; there was widespread dissatisfaction in Germany after Napoleon's conquests, and a yearning to belong to a larger and more massive unit than the small States. Hegel felt this yearning for participation. It had been with him from the first when he was inspired by Rousseau and the ideals of the common life of the Greek city-states. He poured these sentiments into the mould provided by the rise of the new Prussian State. And it was by pronouncements such as these that he did it –

In the existence of a Nation, the substantial aim is to be a State and preserve itself as such. A Nation that has not formed itself into a State – a mere Nation – has strictly speaking no history, like the Nations which existed in a condition of savagery. What happens to a Nation ... has its essential significance in relation to the State ...

And the State inspired Hegel with feelings apparently very similar to those of religion. For example, he had this to say about it –

The State is the Divine Idea as it exists on earth ... We must therefore worship the State as the manifestation of the Divine on earth ... The State is the march of God through the world.

In other words, Hegel's exaltation of the nation provided a semi-mystical backing for his advocacy of State absolutism. In the twentieth century we have suffered too much from these disastrous doctrines to be able to smile too tolerantly at the pompousness with which Hegel expressed them.

Whitehead once said that the world never quite recovers from the shock of a great philosopher. I do not think that Hegel was a great philosopher; but the sheer range and grandiose garrulity of his works acted like a hydrogen bomb on the history of thought – a vast gaseous mushroom cloud settling on the thought of Europe and seeping insidiously into studies and salons. Existentialism, for instance, a movement which has swept the continent since the last war and which is regarded by most English thinkers as a distressing continental aberration, is Hegelian in making an issue of 'existence', in its contempt for 'essence', in its contrast between self and the non-self, its dwelling on the predicament of subjectivity, its 'anguish', and high-sounding talk about Nothingness – all this can be found in Hegel and in his intellectual descendants – Martin Heidegger and Karl Jaspers. Two of the most influential thinkers on aesthetics in modern times, Benedetto Croce in Italy, and R. G. Collingwood in our own country, were avowedly Hegelian. The very subject called the Philosophy of History owes its intellectual origin to Hegel. And it says much for its influence that Karl Popper, one of the most acute of modern philosophers, should think it worth his while to devote a whole book to exposing *The Poverty of Historicism*.

Whether we like it or not, European thought has never been quite the same since Hegel. Even Artur Schopenhauer, who loathed him and all he stood for, could not deny the extent of his influence when he said –

He exerted not only on philosophy alone, but on all forms of German literature, a devastating, or more strictly speaking, a stupefying – one could also say a pestiferous – influence; to combat this influence forcefully and on every occasion is the duty of everybody who is able to judge independently. For if we are silent, who will speak?

There was a man, who, especially in the sphere of political ideas and the interpretation of history, combated Hegel's influence most forcefully – and that was Karl Marx. He was a student of Hegel's who revolted against his master's teaching – he turned Hegel upside-down, to use his own rather picturesque phrase. By this he meant that he substituted matter for Hegel's spirit. But it is seldom realized what an enormous influence the main tenets of Hegel's thought had on Marx's more popular and understandable system.

He took over from Hegel the assumption that there *is* a dialectical development in historical change and that it has an 'essence'. But, in his view, history did not exhibit 'mind clothing itself with the form of events' and developing towards the Absolute. Rather it presented the development of matter – man's efforts to manipulate Nature by techniques of production – and the various forms of social organization which, he claimed, kept pace with these developments by a sort of pre-established harmony. Hegel's conception of nations as dominant expressions of what he called 'the self-developing self-consciousness of the world mind' was transformed by Marx into the conception of social classes fulfilling a historic mission. And just as Hegel thought that the individual's interests and ideals were identical with those of his State, that there could be no morality between States, and that States would constantly be at war with each other; so Marx thought that the individual's interests and ideals were those of his social class, that there could be no morality between classes – the bourgeois, for instance, had quite a different set of principles from those of a member of the proletariat – and that class-war was inevitable, the dynamic of social change. For Hegel history presented a dialectical development of ideas towards the Absolute, a sort of divine argument; for Marx it presented a dialectical development of social change towards a classless society. Marx may have turned Hegel upside-down; but he certainly preserved most of his clothes, into which he poured a more substantial and less gaseous filling.

Some would claim that Marx misused Hegel's ideas; others would claim that he brought them down to earth and made concrete use of them. No one would deny the enormous impact of these ideas on the modern world. The peasant who rebels against his old landlord and the traditions of his family and goes to drive a tractor on a collective farm; the party member who scorns the decencies of civilization and, under unquestionable orders from the Party, wrecks a train or stirs up strife amongst his fellows – such men, perhaps, feel like the Nazis felt, that they are moving on the tide of historical destiny. Such men have abandoned the old gods and put in their place the new gods of nation and class. In so far as any philosopher has a major responsibility for devising these disastrous doctrines, that responsibility must be laid at Hegel's door. Seldom in the history of thought has the influence of a philosopher been quite so out of proportion to his competence or acuteness. Marx said that philosophers have spent too long in trying to understand the world; the point is to change it. His ideas and those of his master, Hegel, have done much to change the modern world. But, in the process, too often something has been sacrificed which has been the perennial goal of philosophers and which is still very highly valued in the West – clarity and truth.

BOOK-LIST

The most relevant writings of Hegel are obtainable in the following editions –

Hegel's Philosophy of Right (translated with notes by T. M. KNOX, Oxford, 1942).

Hegel's Political Writings (translated with notes by T. M. KNOX, Oxford, 1964).

Hegel's Phenomenology of Mind (translated with notes by J. B. BAILLIE, London, revised ed. 1931).

There is a short critical exposition of Hegel's ideas in JOHN PLAMENATZ, *Man and Society*, Vol. II, Chapters 3 and 4 (London, 1963); and a full-length exposition in W. T. STACE, *The Philosophy of Hegel: A Systematic Exposition* (London, 1924: Dover paperback edition, 1955).

Books about Hegel and his philosophy include: C. R. G. MURE, *Introduction to Hegel* (Oxford, 1940); H. MARCUSE, *Reason and Revolution* (London, 1954) and J. N. FINDLAY, *Hegel: A Re-examination* (London, 1958).

II

MAZZINI AND REVOLUTIONARY
NATIONALISM

D. E. D. BEALES

IN 1905 Mahatma Gandhi, who was to be the great prophet, saint and martyr of the Indian national movement of the twentieth century, wrote an article to inform his compatriots about the man who had filled a similar role in the Italian national movement of the nineteenth century, Joseph Mazzini. It is a short article, and most of it is here quoted, because, as well as giving the main facts of Mazzini's life, it is striking evidence of his impact on later nationalists –

Italy as a nation [wrote Gandhi] came into existence recently. Before 1870 Italy comprised a number of small principalities, each with its petty chief. Before 1870, she was like the India ... of today. Though the people spoke the same language and had the same character, they all owed allegiance to different petty states. Today Italy is an independent country and her people are regarded as a distinct nation. All this can be said to be the achievement of one man. And his name – Joseph Mazzini. Joseph Mazzini was born in Genoa on June 22, 1805. He was a man of such sterling character, so good-natured and so patriotic, that great preparations are being made throughout Europe to commemorate the centenary of his birth. For, although he dedicated his whole life to the service of Italy, he was so broadminded that he could be regarded a citizen of every country. It was his constant yearning that every nation should become great and live in unity.

Even at the early age of thirteen Mazzini showed great intelligence. In spite of great scholarship that he evidenced, he gave up his books out of patriotism and undertook the study of law, and began using his legal knowledge gratuitously to help the poor. Then he joined a secret organization which was working for the unification of Italy. When the Italian chiefs learnt of this, they put him in prison. While still in prison, he continued to advance his plans for freeing his country. At last he had to leave Italy ... Though obliged to fly from place to place, he did not lose heart and kept on sending his writings secretly to Italy, which gradually influenced the minds of the people. He suffered a lot in the process. He had to run about in disguise to evade spies. Even his life was frequently in danger, but he did not care ...

In 1848 Mazzini returned ... to Italy, and set up the self-governing State of Italy. It did not last long, thanks to the activities of crafty persons. But, though Mazzini had to flee the country once again, his influence did not fade. The seed of unity that he had sown endured and, though Mazzini remained in banishment, Italy became a single united kingdom in 1870 ...

This great man died in March, 1872. His foes had now become his friends. People had come to recognize his true worth. Eighty thousand people joined his funeral procession ... Today Italy and the whole of Europe worship this man ... He was a pious and religious man, ever free from selfishness and pride. Poverty was for him an ornament. The sufferings of others he regarded as his own. There are very few instances in the world where a single man has brought about the uplift of his country by his strength of mind and his extreme devotion during his own lifetime. Such was the unique Mazzini.*

Gandhi had more to say about who Mazzini was and what he did than about what he thought and wrote. The emphasis is just. Mazzini was more remarkable as a saint and as a revolutionary than as a thinker. Further, in so far as he was a thinker, he was a prophet rather than a philosopher. He explicitly dissociated himself from philosophy. Comparing his own love for Italy with that of more moderate patriots, he said his was *religion*, theirs mere *philosophy*. Unlike all the other men whose ideas are considered in this symposium, he avowed that he was declaring a faith rather than proving propositions, asserting rather than arguing, appealing to the conscience rather than to the intellect; and, unlike them in this also, he was not concerned to analyse politics, but to proclaim a code of behaviour for individuals. This code he observed himself. With Thought,

*The Collected Works of Mahatma Gandhi, Vol. V (1905–06), pp. 27–8: 'Joseph Mazzini', from Indian Opinion, 22 July 1905.

he held, must go Action. For forty years the handsome, soul-ful, guitar-playing aesthete devoted his brain, his energies and his small income to turning out propaganda, organizing revolutionary societies and planning insurrections in the cause of Italian nationalism. His life and deeds spoke louder than his words. Most of those who met him fell under the spell of his personality, as, after his death, did Gandhi. His best-known organization, a society of young revolutionaries, Young Italy, was widely copied, notably by Young Ireland and, later, by the Young Turks. Most nationalist movements, if not necessarily under his direct influence, have employed his methods, which included assassination, terrorism and guerrilla warfare. Dr Nkrumah, indeed, admits to reading him with profit, but he found the works of Marx and Lenin more helpful; Mazzini's theories are woolly and now seem out of date. His practices, however, remain fashionable and effec-tive.

All the same, it is necessary to give some account of his theories. His collected writings fill over a hundred volumes, but he seldom wrote at length, and the most sustained and elaborate statement of his theories is to be found in a short collection of his essays called *The Duties of Man*. It is addressed to the working men of Italy. The point of the title, and the burden of the book, is that there has been too much talk of the rights of individuals, in the tradition of the Enlightenment and the French Revolution, and not enough about their duties. No doubt everyone ought to have rights, but for the mass of the people the granting of legal rights has so far meant little. The material progress of the last century has also passed them by; the profits have gone to the capitalists. The condition of the ordinary man can be improved only by more radical changes. If all would do their duty, then they would become different people, and society as a whole would be transformed. Then rights would be worth having, and spiritual as well as material progress would be open to everyone. Man's duties, which are prescribed by God, are threefold: to Humanity, to his Country, and to his Family. The duty to Humanity comes first. But, for Italians, given their political situation, the most pressing duty is to secure the freedom and unity of their country. Unless this is achieved they can neither do their duty to Humanity nor make social progress. Humanity is too vast, and the individual too weak, for the direct relationship between them to be significant. 'Our Country is our field of labour; the products of our activity must go forth from it for the benefit of the whole earth; but the instruments of labour which we can use best and most effectively exist in it.' Again, as far as social progress is concerned, 'where there is no Country there is no common agreement to which you can appeal; the egoism of self-interest rules alone.' Mazzini sees no difficulty in dividing up the world into nation-states, nor in their co-operating with each other –

God ... divided Humanity into distinct groups upon the face of our globe, and thus planted the seeds of nations. Bad governments have disfigured the design of God, which you may see clearly marked out ... by the courses of the great rivers, by the lines of the lofty mountains, and by other geographical conditions.

Incidentally, of all European countries, Italy is the best-defined by Nature –

The divine design will infallibly be fulfilled. Natural divisions ... will replace the arbitrary divisions sanctioned by bad governments. The map of Europe will be remade. The Countries of the People will rise, defined by the voice of the free, upon the ruins of the Countries of Kings and privileged castes. Between these Countries there will be harmony and brotherhood ... You should have no joy or repose as long as a portion of the territory upon which your language is spoken is separated from the Nation.

But 'a Country is not a mere territory'. A Country, to be a proper Country, must have a single government, wielding undivided authority resulting from the votes of the whole people. It must be republican, because there can be no privilege recognized except that of Genius. Socialism is objectionable, but profits must be shared between Capital and Labour –

The Country ... is the sentiment of love, the sense of fellowship which binds together all the sons of that territory. So long as a single one of your brothers is not represented by his own vote in the development of the national life – so long as a single one vegetates uneducated among the educated – so long as a single one able and willing to work languishes in poverty for want of work – you have not got a Country such as it ought to be, the Country of all and for all.

Italians must dedicate themselves on the one hand to educating and improving themselves and to creating a national consciousness on a basis of true religion, on the other hand to preparing the fundamental revolution by which Italy can be made both politically one and spiritually sublime. It is the mission of Italy, by giving this example, to bring about 'the moral unity of Europe'.

For a few of Mazzini's admirers his whole gospel has been important: he had at one time a considerable following among British Radicals and Free Churchmen as a prophet of an undogmatic, secular and progressive religion. But for most people and for most historical purposes he is simply the archetype of the nationalist, and it hardly matters in detail what his other attitudes were. Still, the general context in which he placed his nationalism is significant. It is common to distinguish two types of nationalist. What is normally regarded as the less pleasant type presses the claims of one particular nation to be great and to dominate over other nations. The extreme representative of this type is Hitler, and it is usual to associate with it Hegel's exaltation of the State, especially the Prussian State, and of war. What is normally regarded as the more pleasant type of nationalist wishes merely that each nation of the world shall have the opportunity to form a State of its own – the principle of self-determination. This view is associated with the desire for peace and international co-operation, with progressive humanitarianism and with liberal democracy. Chiefly through the American President Wilson, it influenced the provisions of the Treaty of Versailles; and Mr Nehru was careful to identify himself with this tradition rather than with that of aggressive, totalitarian nationalism. Mazzini is generally held to belong to the more liberal type – the advocates, as some classify them, of 'nationality' as opposed to 'nationalism'.

In fact Mazzini falls between the two types. He appears liberal in his belief in progress and in the power of education and self-help, in his anticlericalism, his republicanism, his feminism. He acknowledged that some personal liberties, including freedom of opinion, were most valuable. Yet he ranked national unity and equality above liberty, and he thought a nation needed a unifying religion and a unifying system of education. He approached a Hegelian position when he talked of the anarchy of individualism and insisted that 'true Liberty does not consist in the right to choose *evil*, but in the right to choose between the paths which lead to *good*'. In any case, the idea of revolution is difficult to reconcile with liberalism, because the resort to force is the rejection of rational discussion. Mazzini did not entirely avoid making dubious territorial claims under cover of nationalism: he campaigned in the last years of his life for the annexation to the new kingdom of Italy of Nice, Istria and the Trentino.

It is really more appropriate, instead of thinking in terms of two types of nationalist, one more liberal than the other, to think of a continuous gradation among nationalists from Right to Left, from capitalist to communist, from totalitarian democrat to liberal democrat. Although most nationalists confuse this issue, any attempt at a basic definition of nationalism must relate it not to forms of government inside States, but to the determination of the boundaries between States. Nationalists maintain that there exist within Humanity substantial groups which can be distinguished from one another because the members of each have in common certain characteristics or attitudes which the members of the other groups do not share. Probably the criterion most often applied is that of language, but others may be used: race, religion, history. At a minimum it may only be urged that a particular nation be enabled to enjoy some degree of autonomy within a supranational State – as, say, the Scots do within the United Kingdom. But usually it is demanded that each nation – and especially a particular nation – be identified with a State of its own. Right and Left, and almost all the concepts which relate to internal politics, are theoretically irrelevant to this question.

It is true that the idea of democracy is closely bound up with that of a nation, for it is the characteristics and attitudes of the people at large which are supposed to demarcate the nation. But most of Mazzini's attitudes, and those of nationalists in general, are not logically dependent on their nationalism.

It is difficult in practice, though, for any nationalist, however mild in theory, to avoid pressing the claim of a particular nation to dominate over others, if necessary by force. No doubt, if Humanity were actually divided up as nationalists allege it is, they could be thoroughly pacific, internationalist, liberal and humanitarian. But Humanity is not so divided. It is notorious that no criterion of nationality is satisfactory. No pure races exist. Language boundaries are blurred. No religion commands the allegiance of all the inhabitants of one area and of none of the inhabitants of the rest of the world. An individual's consciousness of history is idiosyncratic and highly artificial. In practice none of these criteria of nationality can be reconciled with the territorial definition basic to a State. The Treaty of Versailles ratified the destruction of the greatest multinational or supranational State, the Austrian Empire, but it could only substitute, in the name of self-determination, a group of smaller but still variegated States: Yugoslavia with its Serbs, Croats and Slovenes; Czechoslovakia with its Czechs and Slovaks and its German, Polish and other minorities. It would be impossible to ensure that a State embraced every member of a particular nation and no members of any other nation, except by wholesale deportation or murder, by a ban on immigration and emigration, and by brain-washing with techniques more effective than any so far developed. As long as a nationalist aims, if not at the complete fulfilment of his ideal, at least at a closer approximation to it, he must inevitably wish for territorial adjustments, for restrictions on human rights, for slanted education. The Indian national movement, for example, has been exceptionally anxious to align itself with pacifism, internationalism, liberalism and humanitarianism. But Gandhi and his followers glossed over the great diversity of religions and languages in the sub-continent; they fought bitterly to prevent the creation of the rival nation-state of Pakistan and, after it had been established, to keep it small; in the name of nationalism, but in defiance of treaties, they occupied Goa; and they encourage the teaching only of certain approved Indian languages, discriminating against others and the more generally useful English.

Nationalism, in fact, is an unrealistic doctrine. It is perhaps the kind of doctrine to be expected of intellectuals who are denied the position in society for which their education appears to fit them and who lack the opportunity to acquaint themselves with political realities. In Europe, it was especially characteristic of the romantic, literary-minded intellectuals of the late eighteenth and early nineteenth centuries. During that period, speakers of languages other than French rebelled against its predominance; obsolescent languages were deliberately revived; forgotten literatures were resurrected, some were invented; preposterous assertions were made about the continuity of national traditions and the glories of national pasts. Even in the most genuine cases there was a strong element of rhetoric, myth and fantasy. This approach, brought to bear in politics, leads to curious results. The difference between the ideal on the one hand, and the actual and the practical on the other, is obscured. As with the idea of the General Will and the idea of the dictatorship of the proletariat, so with the idea of the nation. When Italy had been physically united, Mazzini half-disowned the achievement because it did not conform to his ideal: it was monarchical, it recognized privilege, it was scarcely democratic and it ignored the social problem. Nationalism is one example of the tendency in modern thought to multiply Utopias, heavens on earth. In heaven there is, by definition, perfect freedom and concord, and all the good are there gathered together, to the exclusion of all the bad. To aim at attaining this state on earth, though tempting, is mistaken, and often in reality leads to the perversion of the original ideal. Just as the pursuit of perfect freedom and concord on earth has been associated in practice with the suppression of individual liberty and the denial of individual happiness, so the pursuit of nationalism has led to the oppression, sometimes to the extermination, of national minorities. As the historian Acton wrote in prophetic commentary on the unification of Italy: 'the greatest adversary of the rights of nationality is the modern theory of nationality'.

If nationalist politics do not degenerate into repression, they may well degenerate into fatuity. A nation-state must behave as though it is militarily, culturally and economically independent. When this is patently not the case, its politics are liable to enter a world of make-believe. Eire is often cited as the best example. In the shadow of the United Kingdom she cannot be effectively independent. But her politics rest, as they must, on the contrary assumption. There are three main cries. First, Partition must be brought to an end; secondly, the use of the Irish language must be universalized; thirdly, emigration must cease. All three goals are unattainable, if not actually undesirable. Eire has not the military strength to subjugate a reluctant population in Northern Ireland; the English language is better known in Ireland, more useful in the world at large, and more developed than the Irish; and, if the emigrants stayed at home, the Irish economy could not adequately provide for them.

Perhaps the most notable aspect of nationalist unrealism is the refusal to take account of the factor of power. Mazzini reckoned that popular revolution by itself could make Italy. Though many people have assumed that this was what happened, unification was in practice achieved only through the military aid of France in alliance with one of the old Italian states, Piedmont-Sardinia. Mazzini was emphatic that after the initial revolution the nation-state would not employ force, and he visualized a comity of nation-states, sovereign and equal, working together in harmony. This 'sovereign equality' is supposed to characterize the United Nations. Yet sovereignty implies independence, untrammelled by law or morality; and the only practical limitation on the pursuit by sovereign States of their self-interest is the extent of their power. The degree of effective sovereignty varies; the equality is pure fiction. Most political thinkers have neglected the factor of power, but they have often had the excuse that they are dealing with matters of domestic politics, where power is deliberately tamed. Nationalists have no such excuse. Yet their neglect has been little criticized. There was a remarkable demonstration of the reluctance of public men to talk about power at the time of Sir Alec Douglas-Home's speech on the defects of the United Nations Organization in 1961. In a long discussion of this subject on television the point was aired that not all member countries paid their subscriptions, and the point that a country with one million inhabitants or fewer had as many votes in the General Assembly as a country with several hundred million inhabitants. But no one ventured to remark on the anomaly that countries with vast military potential and the power to destroy the whole world had only the same number of votes as countries with virtually no military capacity whatever.

As well as the archetype of the nationalist, Mazzini was notorious as a revolutionary. Ever since the French Revolution progressives have been enchanted, and conservatives horrified, by the possibilities of revolution. But even the French and Russian Revolutions – and certainly lesser movements – have not altered so many things as enthusiasts hoped and reactionaries feared. Mazzini distinguished mere insurrections from true revolution, when men and society would be fundamentally changed. But true revolution is no more an earthly phenomenon than the complete nation-state. Revolutions directed against the international order are in any case particularly unlikely to effect the changes desired, because the factor of power is especially important in this context. But even a purely domestic revolution often goes sour on its promoters. The French Revolution, made in the name of liberty, equality and fraternity, was disfigured by aggressive war and the Terror. The Russian Revolution, which was supposed to be the signal for world revolution, out of which would come peace and the withering away of the State, quickly spawned a militaristic, nationalistic despotism. The use of force to bring down one régime is hardly the best incentive to the abandonment of force by succeeding régimes, which will in any case probably find themselves threatened by new groups of revolutionaries dissatisfied with their achievements.

Mazzini's theories, then, and those of most nationalists, are unrealistic and self-contradictory. But nationalism is still an extremely potent doctrine. It may be asked why so unsound a theory should be so widely held. Two main answers can be given. First, though the full doctrine is absurd, there is, after all, substance in the idea of a nation. Though the only absolutely clear division that can be made between countries is territorial, the linguistic, cultural and religious distinctions, while less precise, are real enough, and much more deeply felt. People do often associate themselves with their compatriots rather than with their fellow men as a whole or even than with the other inhabitants of their locality. Secondly, no régime, given mass communication, can escape making the attempt to be, or at least appear to be, democratic; and a movement for democracy must relate itself to a State, actual or potential. Yet the tenets of democracy are universal in their application: '*All* men are equal . . .' The only theory which reconciles the universalism of the democratic ideal with the actual fragmentation of democracy is nationalism. In a divided world, the idea of the People is naturally accompanied by the idea of the Nation. The ideas of Mazzini live.

BOOK-LIST

The most convenient volume of Mazzini's writings is JOSEPH MAZZINI, *The Duties of Man and Other Essays* (London, Everyman's Library, 1907 or later editions).

On Mazzini's life, *see* BOLTON KING, *The Life of Mazzini* (London, Everyman's Library, 1912); G. SALVEMINI, *Mazzini* (London, 1956). On the Italian nationalist movement in particular, *see* M. SALVADORI, *Cavour and the Unification of Italy* (New York, Anvil Original, 1961); and on nationalism in general the critical study by E. KEDOURIE, *Nationalism* (London, Hutchinson's University Library, 1960).

12

JOHN STUART MILL AND THE
LIBERTY OF THE INDIVIDUAL

J. W. N. WATKINS

MILL's book *On Liberty* was published in 1859, a few months after the death of Mill's wife Harriet. He explained in his *Autobiography* that they had intended to revise it together; but now that she was gone, he would make no further alteration to this work of theirs, which was, he affirmed, 'more directly and literally our joint production than anything else which bears my name, for there was not a sentence of it which was not several times gone through by us together'.

A few years before *On Liberty* was published, Mill had learnt that he had the disease from which his wife was also suffering: consumption. It suddenly seemed that their partnership did not have long to go; and so it became urgent that they should get on paper as many as possible of the ideas which they had long been discussing between themselves. Prominent among these were their ideas on liberty. In the previous year Mill had written an article on liberty and he was now anxious that they should expand this into a book. Such a book, he felt, was badly needed. Liberty had long been under intermittent attack from the right. But to Mill, open attacks on liberty were no longer the main danger. Much more dangerous was the quiet erosion of liberty brought about, largely unintentionally, by moralists and political reformers. 'Almost all the projects of social reformers of these days', he wrote to Harriet, 'are really liberticide.'

Harriet was enthusiastic about the project, and Mill now decided that it was the most important thing they could do 'during the few years of life we have left'. He predicted, correctly, that their projected book 'will make a sensation', adding that 'we must cram into it as much as possible of what we wish not to leave unsaid'.

Like all great political works, *On Liberty* was a response to a danger. Mill had been alerted to this danger many years earlier by Alexis de Tocqueville, in his great book *Democracy in America*.

Tocqueville was not hostile to the growth of social democracy, which he in any case regarded as inevitable; but he perceived in it certain dangerous tendencies, whose general nature is indicated by his phrase 'the tyranny of the majority'. Tocqueville was thinking, primarily, not of democratic *laws* or other overt and deliberate political measures of an illiberal tendency, but of a more subtle kind of tyranny: that exercised by a popular ethos over personal beliefs. Reviewing his book in the *Edinburgh Review*, Mill wrote that he agreed with Tocqueville that the kind of tyranny principally to be dreaded nowadays is one 'not over the body, but over the mind'. Mill went on to claim that the dangerous tendencies which Tocqueville had observed in democratic America were already at work even in England, whose class-ridden social system was far from democratic.

On Liberty takes up Tocqueville's theme in the opening pages. There Mill reiterated that 'the tyranny of the majority' should not be conceived as operating chiefly through the acts of public authorities: a social democracy may practise 'a social tyranny more formidable than many kinds of political oppression, since, though not usually upheld by such extreme penalties, it leaves fewer means of escape, penetrating much more deeply into the details of life, and enslaving the soul itself'.

At the present day, when the *mores* of our society are, with the exception of homosexuals, felt as oppressive by comparatively few people, an effort of historical imagination may be needed to recapture something of the thick moral atmosphere in which middle-class Englishmen lived in Mill's day. The great difference, with regard to political freedom on the one hand and social freedom on the other, between England today and England a hundred years ago, has been nicely described by R. B. McCallum –

If a young man of this age were to find himself back in the eighteen sixties, provided he had some moderate affluence, he would be astounded at the easiness of life and the trifling demands of the state upon him, the light burden of taxation ... He would be free of passports, forms, licenses, regulations. On the other hand, in many matters affecting his private and intellectual life, his love-affairs, his views on religion and science and sex, he would find himself bound by a constricting orthodoxy and would have to guard his words and actions with a care which he might find intolerable.*

Mill conceded that the powerful Victorian ethos, 'our merely social intolerance' as he called it, operated in a quiet and comparatively painless way, achieving its effects without the unpleasant process of fining or imprisoning or killing anybody. It even allowed 'dissentients afflicted with the malady of thought' to exercise their reason, at least in private and provided they disguised their more heterodox opinions from the outside world. It was 'a convenient plan for having peace in the intellectual world, and keeping all things going on therein very much as they do already. But the price paid for this sort of intellectual pacification is the sacrifice of the entire moral courage of the human mind.' This 'yoke of opinion' had, according to Mill, become so heavy that it was really only in commerce and industry that his contemporaries could think and act independently and energetically.

Mill predicted that when democratic majorities have come to feel their power they will be tempted to use it to excess, so that civil liberty will be no less invaded by government action than social liberty had been invaded by social opinion. For my part, I think that this gloomy prediction has hardly been borne out in this country. There was a time when it looked as though it might be. During the 1930s some of the more left-wing socialist thinkers argued that, to forestall counter-revolutionary moves from the right, the first step of a Labour government should be to pass an Enabling Act to enable the party's programme of socialization to be executed swiftly by a

*R. B. McCallum (ed.) On Liberty ... , Introduction, p. xiv (Oxford, 1946).

series of ministerial decrees. This would indeed have been a fulfilment of Mill's prophecy. But in fact, the Labour Government of 1945–51 indulged in no startling departures from constitutional practice. True, the British citizen is more hemmed in by laws and regulations today than he was before the First World War. But he still enjoys more civil liberty than do most citizens in less democratically governed societies in the world today.

So much for the danger which *On Liberty* was designed to combat. Now let us consider the lines along which it tries to combat it. Mill declared that he would not invoke any natural right to Liberty –

I forego any advantage which could be derived to my argument from the idea of abstract right, as a thing independent of utility. I regard utility as the ultimate appeal on ethical questions.

His father, James Mill, had been Bentham's disciple and right-hand man, and Bentham was the founder of the English Utilitarian School. James Mill had personally supervised his son's early education. (Its extraordinary curriculum is described in the opening pages of Mill's *Autobiography*.) Thus the young Mill had been thoroughly indoctrinated with utilitarianism, whose central idea is that everything should be judged according to whether or not it tends to promote the greatest happiness of the greatest number. As a young man, however, John Stuart Mill came, after a severe emotional crisis, to feel that this was too narrow a principle and that it needed to be supplemented by other principles of a more emotionally satisfying character. He never officially forsook the principle of utility. It hovers in the background during his argument for liberty. But in *On Liberty* the principle on which he chiefly and directly relies is a quite different one, which he formulated in this passage –

The object of this Essay is to assert one very simple principle, as entitled to govern absolutely the dealings of society with the individual in the way of compulsion and control, whether the means used be physical force ... or the moral coercion of public opinion. That principle is, that the sole end for which mankind are warranted, individually or collectively, in interfering with the liberty of action of any of their number, is self-protection. That the only purpose for which power can be rightfully exercised over any member of a civilized community, against his will, is to prevent harm to others. His own good, either physical or moral, is not a sufficient warrant.

This 'very simple principle' is not only different from the principle of utilitarianism but, it seems, may even conflict with it: for utilitarianism may oblige us to interfere in situations where Mill's 'very simple principle' would, on the face of it, forbid us to interfere. To give a modern example. If there were a comparatively painless way of preventing people not yet addicted to smoking from acquiring the habit, then (given a causal connexion between smoking and lung cancer) it would be right so to prevent them according to utilitarianism, since prevention would eliminate more misery than it caused. According to Mill's principle, on the other hand, it would presumably be wrong; society would be interfering with people for their own good, rather than to prevent them from harming others.

But, it may be objected, most people who contract lung cancer do thereby cause suffering to others – to their friends, relatives and dependants; thus Mill's 'very simple principle' does not necessarily forbid society from interfering here – not for the good of would-be smokers, but to prevent them causing avoidable suffering to others. This objection points to an important weakness in Mill's principle. He often argues as though adherence to his principle will not only bring important benefits, but will *cost society nothing* (beyond the pangs of frustration felt by indignant busybodies no longer entitled to interfere with the private lives of other people). For he often writes as though the only actions with which society may not interfere are those actions which do not affect society anyway, or which only do so to a negligible extent. It is only, he often seems to be saying, such self-regarding actions – actions which affect only the agent himself – which must not be constrained by society. Indeed, it seems to be not really men's outward actions but only their inward thoughts and feelings that Mill's principle safeguards. The central region of human liberty is, for Mill, 'the inward domain of consciousness'. Here, his principle demands 'liberty of conscience in the most comprehensive sense; liberty of thought and feeling; absolute freedom of opinion and sentiment on all subjects, practical or speculative, scientific, moral or theological'.

We have seen that Mill, at the outset of his essay, laid down the principle of utility as the ultimate yardstick in moral questions; and that he subsequently invoked another principle, not altogether consistent with the first, according to which society must not interfere with an adult person merely for his own good, even if to do so would make him happier (and no one less happy). Later, I shall suggest that what Mill really had in mind was a third principle, not altogether consistent with either of these: the principle, namely, that society should do nothing to hinder men in their pursuit of truth, even though their discoveries may prove dangerous to society. In the meanwhile, let us see how Mill tried to proceed from his 'very simple principle' (which does not appear to safeguard the liberty of an individual when his actions significantly affect other people) to the justification of freedom of speech and publication (despite the fact that what we say and write may affect other people most significantly).

Liberty of discussion is the subject of the second chapter of *On Liberty*, which most people regard as the finest chapter in the book. Mill himself admitted that liberty of discussion is connected somewhat awkwardly with the 'very simple principle' –

The liberty of expressing and publishing opinions may seem to fall under a different principle, since it belongs to that part of the conduct of an individual which concerns other people.

But, Mill argued, liberty of thought and the liberty of expressing and publishing opinions are 'practically inseparable'. Thus Mill gets to the desired conclusion in two steps. His 'very simple principle' demands liberty of private thought; and this in turn demands liberty of public expression.

This seems a shaky justification, however, since the argument can be reversed. An illiberal-minded utilitarian might have replied to Mill along the following lines: 'I entirely agree with you that liberty of thought and liberty of speech and publication are practically inseparable. I also agree with you that society has the right to protect itself against injurious actions. And I think you will agree with me that the publication of certain kinds of books may prove highly injurious to society – only consider how much misery may be caused, indirectly, by the publication a few years ago of *The Communist Manifesto*. I conclude, first that society has the right to exercise a censorship over publishing; and second, in view of the intimate connexion between private thinking and public expressions of thought, that society even has the right to exercise some control over private thinking.'

Mill's 'very simple principle' was hardly strong enough, therefore, to do what he wanted it to do. Let us leave that principle for the present – we will revert to it later – and consider some other independent arguments which Mill gave for liberty of discussion.

He took it for granted that it is good to be in possession of non-trivial truths, and that, other things being equal, a society's well-being improves the larger is its stock of such truths. And he argued that freedom of discussion is essential if the amount of known truth is to increase. His argument went like this: We cannot know of an opinion – outside logic and mathematics, at any rate – that it is true simply by inspecting it. Nor can we rely on any feelings of certainty we may have (an opinion may be false even though we feel certain that it is true). What entitles us to hold an opinion with some confidence can only be the knowledge that it has, so far, withstood searching hostile criticism. Thus even in the case where a received opinion is in fact true, and a heretical opinion opposed to it is false, it would still be a *disservice to truth* to suppress the false opinion: to do so would deprive us of an opportunity to test the true opinion; and the less a true opinion has been tested, the less reason we have for assuming it to be true and the less we appreciate its internal resources, its strength and significance. When truths are protected against criticism they wither into dogmas and intellectual progress slows to a halt: 'Both teachers and learners go to sleep at their post, as soon as there is no enemy in the field.' Moreover, it is irrational to cling to an opinion, even though it happens to be a true opinion, if one is ignorant (or has been kept ignorant) of counter-opinions –

He who knows only his own side of the case, knows little of that. His reasons may be good, and no one may have been able to refute them. But if he is equally unable to refute the reasons on the opposite side; if he does not so much as know what they are, he has no ground for preferring either opinion.

Of course, it may be the heretical opinion which is true and the received opinion which is false – or, what is more usual, both opinions may be partly true and partly false. A public censor would be unable to know in advance whether the received opinion is wholly true, since it is only *after* opinions have been allowed to collide that we can begin to assess their respective strengths and weaknesses. As Mill said –

There is the greatest difference between presuming an opinion to be true, because, with every opportunity for contesting it, it has not been refuted, and assuming its truth for the purpose of not permitting its refutation.

On Liberty was published in the same year as Darwin's *The Origin of Species*; and one might say that Mill regarded the growth of knowledge as a sort of evolutionary process in which true opinions tend to grow stronger and to multiply – provided the struggle for survival is fierce. It was with his idea of intellectual progress towards the truth that Mill backed up these noble declarations at the beginning of the second chapter of *On Liberty* –

The peculiar evil of silencing the expression of an opinion is, that it is robbing the human race; posterity as well as the existing generation; those who dissent from the opinion, still more than those who hold it. If the opinion is right, they are deprived of the opportunity of exchanging error for truth: if wrong, they lose, what is almost as great a benefit, the clearer perception and liveliest impression of truth, produced by its collision with error ...
If all mankind minus one were of one opinion, and only one

person were of the contrary opinion, mankind would be no more
justified in silencing that one person, than he, if he had the power,
would be justified in silencing mankind.

The third chapter of *On Liberty* is entitled 'Of Individuality'. Its message is that each of us should, so to speak, be a
'self-made' man, someone who has formed his own opinions
and worked out his own plan of life, rather than someone
whose opinions are second-hand and who is content to live as
people in his circumstances customarily do. In this context
Mill was prepared to applaud eccentricity, even when it is
indulged in more for its own sake than in pursuit of some
distinctive individual aim: 'In this age the mere example of
non-conformity, the mere refusal to bend the knee to custom,
is itself a service.' Since 'the tyranny of opinion' makes
'eccentricity a reproach', it is good 'that people should be
eccentric'. It will be seen that, although Mill approved of
eccentricity indulged in for its own sake, he valued it, not for
its own sake, but for its custom-disturbing effect. What he
really wanted was not eccentricity as such, but a society in
which each individual leads his own distinctive life according
to his own peculiar talents. Mill's argument here echoes his
argument for the free expression of opinions: the more diversity and contrast there is among individuals' ways of life, the
more progress there is likely to be towards the discovery of
better ways of life –

As it is useful that while mankind are imperfect there should be
different opinions, so it is that there should be different experiments
of living; that free scope should be given to varieties of character,
short of injuries to others; and that the worth of different modes of
life should be proved practically, when anyone thinks fit to try
them. It is desirable, in short, that in things which do not primarily
concern others, individuality should assert itself.

On the whole, Mill's arguments for individuality have
carried less conviction than his arguments for free speech.
Those nineteenth-century readers who felt that rural England
was already being spoilt by the steam-engine, were not very
likely to sympathize with the idea that the village blacksmith,

the parson, and the local farmer should overhaul their habits of thought and re-plan their lives along self-consciously experimental lines.

For my part, whereas I think that Mill's ideas about free speech are essentially right – I should be happy if they prevailed in all places where adult men live together – I consider his idea of individuality valuable rather as a corrective idea which should be heard when contrary ideas prevail, but which should not come to prevail in their stead. Indeed, on Mill's own principles we should not make a religion of individuality. By those principles the climate of moral opinion should be oppressive only for the individual whose actions hurt other people, not for the individual who, without hurting anyone, is not living as bravely and experimentally and distinctively as he might. If someone slips unnoticingly into a customary and inoffensive habit of living then, by Mill's principle of non-interference, we are not entitled to use moral pressure to force him out of it.

I doubt whether Mill really wanted to *goad* people into being individualistic and different; primarily, he wanted to stop people being constrained by public opinion and social pressure into being *un*individualistic and conformist, imitative and dull-minded. I daresay that he would have conceded that his argument for individuality was rather one-sided, in that it hardly acknowledged the immense economies of effort made possible by the existence of ready-made customs which we can take on without having to think out from first principles how to behave in this area. We should indeed remember, as Mill says, 'that nothing was ever yet done which some one was not the first to do, and that all good things which exist are the fruits of originality'. And, we may agree, each of our customary modes of behaving is capable of being improved. But we should also remember that in trying to reform one practice or institution one relies on a great variety of practices and institutions which one is not now seeking to reform. The stability of these other institutions is likely to be indispensable for the rational reform of the institution in question. Similarly, one can break with this custom, and then with that. One cannot simply 'break with custom'. I think that Mill would probably have agreed with this.

If Harriet had not died first, *On Liberty* would have been revised once more before publication. What sort of revision would one have liked them to make?

First, I would have liked them to re-examine their various formulations of that 'very simple principle', their various attempts to draw the line between what must come under the sole sovereignty of the individual and what comes under the purview of society. Sometimes, Mill drew this line between the part of a person's life which concerns only himself ('purely personal conduct', he also calls it) and that which concerns others. Mill himself admitted that some people may find this distinction unworkable. A criticism of it, which was subsequently repeated again and again by Mill's critics, was first voiced by Mill himself –

> How (it may be asked) can any part of the conduct of a member of society be a matter of indifference to the other members? No person is an entirely isolated being; it is impossible for a person to do anything seriously or permanently hurtful to himself, without mischief reaching at least to his near connexions, and often far beyond them ... [And] if by his vices or follies a person does no direct harm to others, he is nevertheless (it may be said) injurious by his example.

So drawn, this distinction appears, as Mill admitted, to allow almost nothing to the individual beyond his sovereignty over his private thoughts and feelings. But usually, as Mr J. C. Rees has emphasized, Mill draws the line between conduct which does not, and conduct which does, affect the *interests* of others prejudicially. This appears to allow rather more to the individual, since conduct may affect other people prejudicially without so affecting their interests. If another man goes off with a young man's girl-friend, that may upset him very much, but it cannot be said to damage his interest in the sense in which the interest of a skilled workman *is* prejudiced if he cannot practise his skill because he has been blackballed by his union. Sometimes Mill goes rather further, drawing the line between conduct which does not, and conduct which does, cause (or threaten to cause) *definite damage* to other people's interests. This again seems to allow rather more to the individual. For example: if someone sells a substantial block of shares, causing the price to fall a few pence, his action would have affected the interests of other shareholders prejudicially, but he could hardly be said to have caused them definite damage.

Let us imagine that Mill had replaced these formulations by one consistent formulation and one which, without departing from his underlying idea, allows most to the individual. Would even this have provided a sufficient basis for his defence of freedom of speech and publication?

I do not think so. Mill himself allowed that there are occasions when freedom of speech may legitimately be circumscribed. It is one thing to publish an article in a newspaper which argues that corn-dealers are starvers of the poor. This, Mill said, ought to be unmolested. It is quite another thing to present that argument in a speech made to an excited mob assembled before the house of a corn-dealer. This latter action, Mill judged, 'may justly incur punishment'.

But suppose that the publication of a certain book may reasonably be expected to lead, after a time-lag, to much more serious damage than would have been caused by the speech outside the corn-dealer's house: would not society be justified, on Mill's principles, in suppressing such a book? Or consider the series of scientific papers which made possible the construction of an atom-bomb: should not they have been suppressed?

I said earlier that Mill relies, in his argument for liberty, on three separate principles: the principle of utility; the principle of non-interference with self-regarding conduct (self-regarding conduct being complementary to interest-prejudicing, or interest-damaging, conduct); and what may be called the pursuit-of-truth principle (that the suppression of any opinion, whether true or false, is a disservice to truth). I am persuaded that his first two principles were not strong enough, separately or conjointly, to support his case, and that he actually weakened it by relying on them. Suppose that he had attained a certain distance from those two principles, viewing them as interesting approximations, of considerable value but somewhat defective. How then might he have justified rejection of the proposal that politically dangerous writings like *The Communist Manifesto*, or technologically dangerous writings like those of Einstein, Bohr, Frisch and others should be censored? Perhaps along the following lines: 'The pursuit of truth is a risky undertaking. It may yield large benefits to society. It may also create great dangers. And we cannot so control men's inquiries that they yield the benefits without the dangers. So we must either abandon the pursuit of truth, or accept the risks it involves. But even if it were possible, it would be beneath human dignity to abandon the pursuit of truth for the sake of security. Let us not suppose (as the unrevised wording of *On Liberty* might lead one to suppose) that liberty costs nothing. Let us recognize that it may prove very costly; and let us affirm that we are willing to pay the cost.'

Yet we should remember that Mill's aim was to *argue* a case for liberty, to argue it cogently and soberly; and when someone is arguing for the principle he values most, something rather perverse tends to occur. He cannot argue for principle *A* merely by affirming *A*; he has to appeal to *other* principles, say *B* and *C* . . .; but if *A* is what he values most, he values *B* and *C* less highly: the superior principle is justified by inferior principles; and these may not prove quite good enough to justify it effectively. I suspect that something like this happened in Mill's argument for liberty, thereby producing the anomalies we have noticed.

But *On Liberty*, warts notwithstanding, is still an important book, especially for democrats. It exposes certain 'liberticide' tendencies incipient within a political and social democracy; and it thereby helps us to contain those tendencies.

BOOK-LIST

The relevant writings of Mill include –

MILL, J. S., *On Liberty and Representative Government* (ed. R. B. Mc-Callum, Oxford, 1946).

MILL, J. S., *Autobiography* (Oxford, World's Classics, 1924 and later editions).

MILL, J. S., *The Earlier Letters ... 1812 to 1848* (Collected Works, ed. F. E. Mineka, Vols. XII–XIII, 1963).

MILL, J. S., *Mill on Bentham and Coleridge* (ed. F. R. Leavis, Cambridge, 1950).

Books about Mill include –

ANSCHUTZ, R. P., *The Philosophy of J. S. Mill* (Oxford, 1953).

HAYEK, F. A., *John Stuart Mill and Harriet Taylor* (London, 1951).

PACKE, M. ST. J., *The Life of John Stuart Mill* (London, 1954).

REES, J. C., *Mill and his Early Critics* (London, 1956).

13

MARX AND MODERN CAPITALISM

P. H. VIGOR

KARL MARX was born at Treves in Germany in 1818, the son of a Jewish lawyer who later became Christian. He became involved in political activity early in his life; and in 1848, the year in which there were serious revolts in most of the kingdoms of Europe, Marx publicly urged that the people of Cologne should not pay the taxes imposed upon them by the Prussian Government. He was tried for sedition, but acquitted by the jury. Later, however, he was expelled by the authorities; whereupon he came to England, where he lived until his death in 1883, still preoccupied with politics and with political writing.

His great work was *Das Kapital*, which he did not succeed in finishing before he died; it was Engels who completed it from the notes which Marx had left. But though *Das Kapital* is perhaps his greatest work, *The Communist Manifesto* has been probably the more widely read. It is a short, emotive work, a call to revolutionary activity; and Marx wrote it in 1847 in conjunction with Engels and published it in that same year of 1848, that year of the revolutions, in which Marx was expelled from his homeland.

These, and his other works, stand a little apart from those of the other philosophers who are included in this series. They all concerned themselves exclusively with one or another aspect of what we would call 'politics'; but though Marx spent all his life in political activity, for him, politics and political science were, in a sense, secondary affairs; their form was determined, and their evolution hastened or retarded, by the economic system which gave rise to them. In other words, economics was the basic factor which governed everything; it governed religion, it governed morality, and it also governed politics. Here are some paragraphs from *The Communist Manifesto* which give the essence of his thought upon the subject. He is talking about the rise of capitalism. Incidentally, the word 'manufacture', which occurs several times in this passage, must be understood in its original sense of 'making things by hand, or by hand-operated tools' –

The feudal system of industry, under which industrial production was monopolized by closed guilds, now no longer sufficed for the growing wants of the new markets. The manufacturing system took its place. The guild-masters were pushed on one side by the manufacturing middle class; division of labour between the different corporate guilds vanished in the face of division of labour in each single workshop.

Meantime the markets kept ever growing, the demand ever rising. Even manufacture no longer sufficed. Thereupon, steam and machinery revolutionized industrial production. The place of manufacture was taken by the giant, Modern Industry, the place of the industrial middle class, by industrial millionaires, the leaders of whole industrial armies, the modern bourgeois.

Modern industry has established the world market, for which the discovery of America paved the way. This market has given an immense development to commerce, to navigation, to communication by land. This development has, in its turn, reacted on the extension of industry; and in proportion as industry, commerce, navigation, railways extended, in the same proportion the bourgeoisie developed, increased its capital, and pushed into the background every class handed down from the Middle Ages.

We see, therefore, how the modern bourgeoisie is itself the product of a long course of development, of a series of revolutions in the modes of production and of exchange.*

Now, it is clear that a man with a cast of mind like that will have little in common with Rousseau or Burke or Mill. Not that Marx evolved his theories without any help from anyone: all men, however eminent, are influenced in their thinking by one or another of those who have gone before them. But the men who influenced Marx were men like Hegel, Feuerbach, Fourier and Saint-Simon, men of whom the public has scarcely heard; so that, in our eyes, Marx seems to stand

The Communist Manifesto.

apart from other thinkers – not because he does so in reality, but because he derived from a school of thought of which we in Britain usually know so little.

The basic stuff of all human history consists, in Marx's view, of the two principles of 'class' and 'exploitation'.

Under modern capitalism there are three 'classes', in the Marxist sense of the word: there are those who employ labour; there are those who are employed; and there is a third class (relatively small and unimportant today) consisting of one-man businesses. These 'classes' are the only groups or classifications of men which Marx considered important; and he saw each class as being united within itself by the fact that it has a common economic interest. Thus, the economic interest of the employers (whom Marx termed the 'bourgeoisie') is to get as much work out of their employees as possible, while paying them as little as they can. Conversely, the economic interest of the wage-earners (whom Marx called the 'proletariat') is to get as much money from their employers as they can, while doing the minimum in return for it.

In other words, the class interests of the two main classes are, Marx thought, fundamentally irreconcilable; and it is this which makes inevitable in any class society, such as capitalism, the existence of a class-struggle – that is to say, of a kind of non-stop civil war, with all the attendant waste and misery and frustration which this causes.

The misery and frustration of the class-struggle are deepened among the workers by the knowledge that they are victims of exploitation; and by 'exploitation' Marx meant the difference between the value of what a worker produces and the amount of money he gets paid for doing so. Obviously, there is such a difference; otherwise, there would be no point in employing labour; but whereas most people accept this as just one of the facts of life, it was in Marx's view an appalling and far-reaching evil, against which the workers would ultimately come to revolt.

This tendency of theirs to revolt would be intensified, in his opinion, by the operations of the boom-slump cycle. This was an undoubted characteristic of capitalist society right up to the Second World War, and caused an enormous amount of misery. The hunger marches, the depressed areas, the million or more of our labour force who, year after year, continued to be unemployed, are well-known and eloquent testimony to the evils of a slump.

But then, during the Second World War, there came about a general acceptance of the economic theories of Lord Keynes, the substance of which was that the boom-slump cycle and mass unemployment are avoidable. As a result, every government which has been returned to power since the war ended has been pledged to prevent the recurrence of any such thing.

'But have they?' Marx might say if he were alive now: 'Oh, I know', he would go on, 'that all these Governments have indeed been *pledged* to prevent the return of a slump. But have they actually succeeded in doing so? Don't you talk a lot about stop-go policies; and what are these but the boom-slump cycle under another name? Admittedly, the depression is not nearly as severe as it used to be in the old days, if you take the country as a whole; but it's a fat lot of consolation to an unemployed shipwright on Tees-side to know that those in the South-East have never had it so good.'

Moreover, not only the unemployed shipwright on Tees-side, but the whole of the proletariat, would come to realize that their situation was getting worse. Not that Marx denied that the standard of living of the workers might quite possibly go up, but he said that that of the bourgeois would go up faster. He also said (quite rightly) that rich and poor are purely relative terms. In Elizabethan times, you were a rich man if you had a proper bed; today, you are a pauper if you have not got one. A hundred years ago, it was a luxury to have a proper bathroom; today, houses are being condemned as substandard because they are without them. The working-man of the second half of the twentieth century is certainly likely to have a house, electric light, main drainage, hot and cold water, good clothes, good furniture, a washing machine, and probably a motor-car; and this makes him infinitely better off than the working-man of a hundred years ago.

'But has not the modern capitalist', Marx would say, 'got

even richer still? Doesn't he have a town house and a country house, two or three cars, a yacht, and perhaps an aeroplane, and the means to go off to the Caribbean or the South of France whenever the whim takes him? And isn't this a bigger gap than that which existed between capitalist and worker in Victorian times?'

I am not sure that Marx was right on this point. The Victorian capitalist may not have had an aeroplane or a motor-car, but thanks to plentiful servants and low taxation, he lived in conditions of probably the most solid comfort that the world has ever seen. On the other hand, it is impossible to say (and quite impossible to prove) whether the gap between him and the Victorian worker was less or greater than that between their modern equivalents, or whether it was about the same. If Marx was right, the gap between them was less during his life-time and has steadily widened since; and this ever-widening gap was to be another cause of fury and frustration for the workers.

Moreover, there was, Marx thought, a defect in the working of capitalism which he called 'the crisis of over-production'. Factories, as we all know, cannot work profitably unless they are working more or less flat out. This causes a huge volume of goods to be deposited on the market, and this, in turn, calls for a high level of demand; for unless there are customers to buy the goods as they come off the assembly lines, the market will be choked and the factories will have to stop.

In Marx's view, not enough people had enough money to buy the goods which were produced; and consequently there would be over-production. He pointed out that this was over-production only in relation to the amount of cash available: in a world in which many people were hungry and in rags, there was plenty of *need* for the goods; the trouble was that those who were in need had not the money to buy. Here is an extract from *Das Kapital* about this –

It is not a fact that too many necessities of life are produced in proportion to the existing population. The reverse is true. Not enough is produced to satisfy the wants of the great mass decently and humanely.

It is not a fact that too many means of production are produced to employ the able-bodied portion of the population. The reverse is the case. In the first place, too large a portion of the population is produced consisting of people who are really not capable of working. who are dependent through force of circumstances on the exploitation of the labour of others, or compelled to perform certain kinds of labour which can be dignified with this name only under a miserable mode of production. In the second place, not enough means of production are produced to permit the employment of the entire able-bodied population under the most productive conditions, so that their absolute labour time would be shortened by the mass and effectiveness of the constant capital employed during working hours.

On the other hand, there is periodically a production of too many means of production and necessities of life to permit of their serving as means for the exploitation of the labourers at a certain rate of profit. Too many commodities are produced to permit of a realization of the value and surplus-value contained in them under the conditions of distribution and consumption peculiar to capitalist production, that is, too many to permit of the continuation of this process without ever-recurring explosions.

It is not a fact that too much wealth is produced. But it is true that there is periodical overproduction of wealth in its capitalistic and self-contradictory form.

As great a defect in capitalism in Marx's eyes was what he termed 'the reserve army of unemployed'; for unless there were large numbers of men without jobs, capitalism, he maintained, could not possibly function.

This, at any rate, is one point about which Marx was clearly wrong, was he not? In America and Canada there may still be a high rate of unemployment; but, at all events, in Britain we have full employment – which shows that capitalism *can* do away with unemployment, if it really wants to. .

This may be true. Nevertheless, Marx, if he were alive today, would probably not be satisfied. One function of the reserve army of unemployed, in his opinion, was to act as a pool of labour on which capital could draw every time that a boom was in the offing; and without such a pool, he thought, no boom could possibly materialize, as the expanding economy would not have the extra labour necessary to service its expansion.

The British economy since the end of the Second World War has experienced a number of booms. Whenever this happens, new industries start up, and old ones build more plant and go on to extensive overtime to meet their orders. Where does the labour for all this come from? Does it not come from the many thousands who were unemployed during the preceding recession?

It can be argued that these thousands of unemployed are only a temporary phenomenon, the product of an economic depression which itself is transient; but this is not a point that Marx would ever have disputed. He would have agreed that every slump comes to an end some time or other, but would have denied that this affected his main contention. And is it, indeed, possible to maintain that we have no booms and slumps (in a modified form) today; or that, as far as labour is concerned, the booms still rely on the slumps?

'Nor is the argument refuted', Marx would go on, 'by saying that to have a boom, you don't need to have a slump; by saying that you can have a boom, and go on from there to have a super-boom. Of course you can. And where does the labour for the super-boom come from? It comes from the unemployed of Pakistan, Africa, and the West Indies. As soon as business over here finds it impossible to get workers, the management applies to the Ministry of Labour to issue work permits – to allow sufficient workers in to fill the vacancies that otherwise stay vacant. And do these workers come to this cold, damp country, if they have good jobs in their own countries? Of course not. Those who come are those who have no job, and, what is more, little prospect of getting one. The reserve army of unemployed may be an international, rather than a purely national body; but it still seems that capitalism cannot function without it.'

When we, who live under capitalism, think of Marx, our minds are naturally full of his strictures upon our form of society; but, of course, if you read *Das Kapital*, you will see that, as well as condemning capitalism, he also praised it. As compared with feudalism or slavery, he said, it was on the whole a beneficent system; it had greatly increased the productive powers of man; the wealth it had created had allowed a start to be made on eradicating evils which, up to its advent, had seemed to be part of the basic stuff of human existence. Only, said Marx, it was now a prisoner of its own characteristics; the things that most needed doing in the world could not, by the very nature of capitalism, be done under capitalism; since capitalism, which was impelled by profit, would produce only those things it could hope to sell at a profit, and only at times when it was profitable to do so –

One capitalist always kills many. Hand in hand with this central-ization, or this expropriation of many capitalists by few, develop, on an ever extending scale, the co-operative form of the labour-process, the conscious technical application of science, the method-ical cultivation of the soil, the transformation of the instruments of labour into instruments of labour only usable in common, the economizing of all means of production by their use as the means of production of combined, socialized labour, the entanglement of all peoples in the net of the world-market, and with this, the inter-national character of the capitalistic régime. Along with the con-stantly diminishing number of the magnates of capital, who usurp and monopolize all advantages of this process of transformation, grows the mass of misery, oppression, slavery, degradation, exploit-ation; but with this too grows the revolt of the working-class, a class always increasing in numbers, and disciplined, united, or-ganized by the very mechanism of the process of capitalist produc-tion itself. The monopoly of capital becomes a fetter upon the mode of production, which has sprung up and flourished along with, and under it. Centralization of the means of production and socialization of labour at last reach a point where they become incompatible with their capitalist integument. This integument is burst asunder. The knell of capitalist private property sounds. The expropriators are expropriated.*

In other words, in Marx's view, capitalism had had its day. The new technological processes, gestating in the womb of time, would need a less chaotic, less tribal, less blindly com-petitive economic organization, if they were to be born and

Capital, Vol. 1, Chapter 32.

prosper. In the Middle Ages, each city had its own customs service and levied tolls upon all who entered it: which was still true in the time of Machiavelli. The growth of trade and industry made such arrangements anachronisms. They were a fetter on the growth of the economy, which the strength of the growing economy finally snapped.

So it would be with capitalism. These petty firms, these futile divisions of the world into individual sovereign states, are they not just as much a brake upon the development of the economy, as independent cities such as Machiavelli's Florence had been in their day? And how would capitalism, which was based upon competition and self-seeking, end such anarchy and introduce the planning and social discipline which the new technology would need?

Our own day has provided no clear answers to these questions. On the one hand, some of the most modern industries, such as atomic energy and space research, are in government hands, even in the most capitalist countries; and this might seem to be a justification of Marx, as might the fact that all governments nowadays indulge in at least *some* planning. On the other hand, in 1963, it seemed clear that Marx was wrong about the frontiers, and that all of western Europe was going to merge into one Common Market. Then President de Gaulle forbade the British entry; and it seemed that, after all, Marx had been right, and that, at the last fence, the capitalist horse would refuse. Thereafter it was impossible to say whether, on this particular issue, Marx was right or wrong. Were we, perhaps, merely in the middle of a pause, after which Britain *will* join the Common Market? Or would the Six continue to remain the Six, and Britain look west-wards and enter into some sort of partnership with America? Or could it turn out to be perfectly good economics for the present fragmented patchwork of Europe to continue; and for those national frontiers and lack of planning, which Marx saw as a fetter upon production, to be in reality no such thing?

These were not the only defects which Marx detected in capitalism. He believed that the rate of profit would, in the long run, fall to such a level that capitalism would no longer be able to operate; he believed that, as time went on, capital would be concentrated into fewer and fewer hands, and that this unbalance of monetary resources would be another one of the causes of capitalism's downfall: he believed that capitalists are warmongers. These defects, and the ones already mentioned – the need of capitalism to have in existence a reserve army of unemployed; the resentments caused by unemployment, by 'exploitation' and by the steadily widening gap between the standards of living of the 'bourgeois' and the 'proletariat'; the existence of the 'class-struggle'; the 'boom-slump' cycle; the crisis of over-production; and, as compared with communism, its technological inefficiency – these would be sufficient to undermine capitalism's foundations.

In this connexion, the role of the Trade Unions becomes a factor of great importance. Marx himself, however, paid little attention to them. Even in England, they did not become legal until 1871; and Marx died only twelve years later. His theories had been evolved by then, his cast of mind set. Here is the only passage in his writings in which he gives the Trade Unions more than a passing mention. It comes from his *Wages, Price and Profit* published in 1865 –

Trades Unions work well as centres of resistance against the encroachments of capital. They fail partially from an injudicious use of their power. They fail generally from limiting themselves to a guerrilla war against the effects of the existing system, instead of simultaneously trying to change it, instead of using their organized forces as a lever for the final emancipation of the working class, that is to say, the ultimate abolition of the wages system.

It is over eighty years since Marx died, which makes it necessary to raise the question of his relevance to modern capitalism. As you do so, will you please keep in mind the following three questions; for it is on the answers to these that, as it seems to me, Marxism must be judged –

(i) Are the defects which Marx noted still to be found in the capitalism of our day?

(ii) If so, are they still sufficiently serious to constitute a threat to capitalism's existence? Or have they either been eliminated, or so damped down as to be no danger to the system? Few even of the apologists for capitalism would claim that it is perfect; but many say that it has adjusted itself sufficiently to enable it to survive. Do you agree?

(iii) In any case, although of course capitalism may break up simply through functional instability, there is no point in destroying it *intentionally*, unless you have something better to put in its place. Marx thought that he had. He was quite certain (and thought he had scientifically proved) that in his ideal society of communism there would be no 'class struggle', 'exploitation', over-production or any of the other evils of capitalism listed on the preceding pages.

He ends the second edition of *The Communist Manifesto* with these words –

When, in the course of development, class distinctions have disappeared, and all production has been concentrated in the hands of a vast association of the whole nation, the public power will lose its political character. Political power, properly so called, is merely the organized power of one class for oppressing another. If the proletariat during its contest with the bourgeoisie is compelled, by the force of circumstances, to organize itself as a class, if, by means of a revolution, it makes itself the ruling class, and, as such, sweeps away by force the old conditions of production, then it will, along with these conditions, have swept away the conditions for the existence of class antagonisms and of classes generally, and will thereby have abolished its own supremacy as a class.

In place of the old bourgeois society, with its classes and class antagonisms, we shall have an association, in which the free development of each is the condition for the free development of all.

Perhaps he was right? But perhaps his 'proof' was merely a terminological one? You may get rid of the class struggle in the Marxist sense, and still find that men will persist in quarrelling. You may, in any case, get rid of one set of evils, only to find that you have been landed with a lot of others. 'You kick the polecat out of the kitchen window, only to find the skunk crawl in at the door.' That little aphorism is not Mr Khrushchev's, but one of mine; though I am prepared to sell it to the late Soviet leader for a suitable fee. It does, however, express what seems to me to be a truth about life with which you may agree: equally, of course, you may disagree with me and agree with Marx instead.

Marx, naturally, had no doubts about the correctness of his own view, and was prepared to do all that he could in order to achieve communism. As it so happened, though, it was not he who actually made the Revolution in a European country; that was done by Lenin. But Lenin, though he based himself on Marx, had to add to Marxism certain tools and tactics in order to attain the goal that Marx had set.

BOOK-LIST

MARX, K. and ENGELS, F., *The Communist Manifesto* (ed. W. Reeves).

MARX, K., *Capital* (Everyman's Library).

MARX, K. and ENGELS, F., *Selected Works*, 2 vols. (London, 1950 or later editions).

Marx on Economics, ed. ROBERT FREEDMAN (Pelican book, 1963), is a selection of extracts on economic matters taken from a number of his writings. On Marx himself *see* ISAIAH BERLIN, *Karl Marx: his Life and Environment* (Oxford, Home University Library, 1939 or later editions); and on Marxism, JOHN PLAMENATZ, *German Marxism and Russian Communism* (London, 1954) and R. N. CAREW HUNT, *The Theory and Practice of Communism: An Introduction* (London, 1950; Penguin Books, 1964).

14

RECENT POLITICAL THOUGHT

A. C. MACINTYRE

MOST previous writers of these chapters have been able to put a single thinker in the centre of their stage. It is one of the distinctive marks of the present age that I cannot hope to do that. Political theory has not only become too complex and varied in its subject-matter, but it has also had a tortuous history of its own. It is only a decade or so since its death was being confidently announced in some quarters, a death that was felt by those who announced it to be a welcome relief. They saw the past of political theory as a series of metaphysical confusions which positivist philosophy had now revealed to be linguistic muddles. Moreover in practice the theories which had dominated the thirties, those of Stalinism and Fascism, appeared not only to be conceptually confused but also to be dangerous and vicious in their practical consequences. How much sounder and safer it seemed to be able to welcome the end of ideology and to return to a comfortable and comforting English empiricism – to drop the theory and remain close to the facts. Henceforward the fact-gathering discipline of political science would replace the imaginative flights of political theory.

As it turned out, these obituary notices were premature. For one thing, the notion that politics could be conducted without theory was itself all too plainly a theory. But more than this two quite independent influences combined to show how necessary political theory is. The first influence was that of empirical political science. Here as in other sciences fact-gathering only becomes fruitful if it is part of the process of framing hypotheses and explanations, and of testing them. All the multifarious pieces of information we now have about voting behaviour, for example, only become of use and interest in so far as they help us understand the nature and possibilities of alternative voting systems; and to understand this is to theorize. The second influence is that of political practice; politicians continue to use theories not only to understand and to explain, but also as instruments and weapons. And the way in which they use theories suggests the need for a theory about theories.

We can begin from the 'Cold War' confrontations of the Soviet Union and the West. The most familiar criticisms of the Russian social and political system have been first of all that it is inimical to freedom because it does not embody the canons of parliamentary democracy, and moreover that it could not but be inimical to freedom because it was fathered by Marxists. In other words, the Russian reality is confronted by John Stuart Mill's ideals and fails the test; while the explanation of this failure is that within Marxism the seeds of unfreedom always lay and lie. We are thus plunged straightaway into contentions about theory. Nobody could deny that John Stuart Mill would be unhappy about even post-Khrushchevite Russia; but is this the best clue we have to the nature of Russian unfreedom?

To answer this question I begin with another and ask why Marxist theory should be accused of having fathered Stalinist tyranny. Of the many arguments that have been used two perhaps deserve special notice. The first is the accusation that Marxism is wedded to a view of history which necessarily leads to totalitarianism. The Marxist, so it is said, believes in inevitable trends in history. He believes that he and his party are the contemporary representatives of those trends and are thus justified by historical necessity in depriving their opponents of liberty and even of life. But Marxism, so it has been suggested, is mistaken, simply because there are no such trends. It was Karl Popper, the philosopher of science, who named all those who believe in such unconditional and inevitable trends in history 'historicists'. Historicists do not see, so he argued, that the existence of any historical trend depends upon initial conditions – and that these conditions may not persist, may be alterable.

Not only Marx, but other nineteenth-century philosophers such as Auguste Comte, so Popper suggested, have been in danger of being the victims of confusion in ignoring the difference between absolute and unconditional *prophecies* of the future and the conditional *predictions* of the scientist – precisely because they have ignored the initial conditions of the trends they claimed to discern –

The point is that these conditions are so easily overlooked. There is, for example, a trend towards an 'accumulation by means of production' (as Marx puts it). But we should hardly expect it to persist in a population which is rapidly decreasing; and such a decrease may in turn depend on extra-economic conditions, for example, on a chance invention, or conceivably on the direct physiological (perhaps biochemical) impact of an industrial environment.

So Popper in *The Poverty of Historicism*.

But did Marx in fact confuse prophecy and prediction? His use of words like 'inevitable' certainly suggests a belief in irresistible unconditional trends. Yet such a belief is, for example, incompatible with Marx's own picture of the working class intervening to put an end to the trends of capitalist development by altering the conditions on which their continuation depends. That Marx is not wholly conceptually clear seems undeniable. That he is totally and necessarily committed to what is genuinely fallacious in historicism seems less clear.

A second type of argument used by other recent critics of Marx is that Marxism is committed to the notion of a centralized, undemocratic revolutionary party with an iron inner discipline which in the name of democracy is to impose upon the masses not what the masses say they want, but what the party knows that they really want, irrespective of what they may say. Marxism, so it was asserted, had inherited the tradition of such a party from the Jacobins in the French Revolution, who had in turn been influenced by Rousseau. So once again theory was seen as lying at the root of political error.

It is therefore fascinating that when in 1956–7 there was

widespread revolt against the established authorities in eastern
Europe, it was from Marxism – according to its western
critics the source of the tyranny – that many of the leaders of
the revolt drew their inspiration. The mechanistic picture of
historical inevitability which western critics identified with
Marxism they identified with the Stalinist corruption of
Marx's thought. So too with the dogmas of the dictatorial
party. Instead they stressed Marx's concern with freedom. The
ambiguous formulae of traditional Marxism, which can be
read in several ways, were reinterpreted in the light of the
rediscovered libertarianism especially of the younger Karl
Marx. The Polish philosopher, Lescek Kolakowski, argued
against historicism as powerfully as Popper had done, but in
the name of Marxism. The Polish sociologist, Stanislaw
Ossowski, treated the Marxist theory of class-structure and
class-struggle as a contribution to sociology to be judged by
ordinary scientific standards. But in the course of this liberation of Marxism from its own dogmatism a new question
came to be formulated.

The West had insisted that the Soviet Union failed if
judged by the standards of Mill's liberalism. To some thinkers
in the East this seemed not the most relevant standard;
what they urged was that the Soviet Union should be judged
by the standards of its own professed doctrines. How, they
inquired, would Russian society look if it was seen in the
light of the Marxist perspective which the Russians themselves
claimed to use to criticize the West? To American claims
that America is a classless society, in spite of the wide differences in income, because there is openness of opportunity,
the Russian reply was that the wide differences in income
reflect wide differences in power, and that these are rooted in
a class-structure in which the opportunity to move from one
class to another does nothing to diminish the existence of
classes. But in Soviet society we find wide income differences
too – what do these reflect? Mere functional differences in the
usefulness of certain sorts of job, reply the apologists for the
status quo in Russia. But this after all is what apologists for the
American *status quo* say of inequality in the U.S.A. Ossowski

in his *Class Structure in the Social Consciousness* noted this and went on to frame an answer which he was prudent enough to put into the mouths of *émigré* anti-Soviet intellectuals. He first points out that in general Marxist methods – because they threaten established stereotypes and social fictions – are not used by the privileged and the established, but by the hostile outsider. Some Soviet *émigrés*, and, so he might have added, some of Trotsky's later western followers, let alone a critic like Djilas, have tried to show how in Russia a new class structure has been formed. Ossowski writes –

... those who like to apply Marxian methods to Soviet society in the Stalinist period stress the wide range of wage-scales and the importance of such economic privileges as were not included in the total of monetary rewards. They try to emphasize the tendency to stabilize class differences, citing such features as the great reduction in death duties and the sliding scale for income tax introduced in 1943; the reintroduction of fees for secondary and higher education in 1940, which was confirmed by the amendment of the 121st article of the Stalinist constitution in 1947; the system of rights, subsidies, privileges, and so on. In general, they attempt to apply the Marxian theory of the state to the Soviet state.

Ossowski restricts his account to the Stalinist period. But for all the liberalization of post-Stalin Russia the critics could still point to the entrenchment of hierarchy and privilege.

It is for this reason that the very theory, which the Russians try to project outwards on to the western world, they cannot allow to be used for the study of their own society – or else the realities of their own state capitalism and of their treatment of their own working-class would stand revealed. And it is not only Marx whom they have to fear, it is Lenin too. Writing only two months before October 1917 Lenin had discussed the organization of the early phases of the new revolutionary society, in terms of the most democratic and egalitarian strain in Marxism. He envisaged every citizen participating in the administration of the State. Capitalism, so he believed, had simplified accounting and control to the point where every literate worker could participate without difficulty in government: 'The whole of society will have become a single office and a single factory, with equality of labour and equality of pay.'

Lenin himself certainly never managed remotely to embody the ideals of *State and Revolution* in the young Soviet state. But so long as his writings are canonized in the Soviet Union there is a deep incompatibility between what the Soviet theorists are forced to admit about what ought to be the case in Russia, if Marxist-Leninism really prevailed, and the way that they themselves live as part of the privileged ruling-class bureaucracy.

I have tried to bring out the contrast between the proclaimed political ideals of the Soviet Union and the truth which their own official political theory would reveal if they applied it to themselves. But we must ask if it is only of Russia that this is true? In an even sharper form we find a similar contrast in the West where established political theory and established political ideals contradict each other in the most violent way. Our established political ideals are those of parliamentary liberalism; we believe officially in a society in which the people choose their rulers by free and responsible majority vote after having considered the merits of the alternative policies of rival candidates on the basis of both past records and future projects. Equality of opportunity, it is asserted, although admittedly imperfectly realized, means that almost everyone has at least some chance to participate at the level he wishes to in the political process. What is interesting is that no other single theme has so engaged western political theory as the attempt to show that this ideal is never realized, that people *cannot* rule themselves, that ruling in politics and management in industry are necessarily the specialized function of minority *élites*, and that inequality is a political and social necessity. 'The formula "Government of the people by the people" must be replaced by this formula: "Government of the people by an *élite* sprung from the people" ', writes Professor Duverger, the French expert on *élite* theory when he comes in his great book, *Political Parties*, to express the nearest possible approximation to democracy that one might realistically aspire to. But an *élite* sprung from the people is still an *élite* and an *élite* quickly becomes professionalized. So Schumpeter wrote cruelly and truthfully 'that democracy is the rule of the politicians'.

Why must politicians and managers rule? One form of argument in *élite* theory would begin by trouncing what would be seen as the naïveté of Lenin's view of administration in the passage quoted earlier. Administration, man-management, involves the use of varied and difficult skills. A society or a factory can only be run along the grooves of social order. A much more interesting form of argument turns on the analysis of what any system of parties and electors *must* become. Parties become in-groups, elections become occasions when rival minorities solicit the electorate, and the electorate plays a passive rather than an active role in its choices. This kind of theory was first formulated over half a century ago by writers such as G. Mosca and R. Michels in the light of experiences of the transformation of popular movements and working-class parties in Europe, such as the German social democrats, into machines dominated by full-time officials and working politicians. It has been extended by American sociologists to explain the detail of politics in a variety of situations. It is summarized in another aphorism of Schumpeter's that democracy is a system 'in which individuals acquire the power to decide by means of a competitive struggle for the people's vote'. The people constitute not the sovereign power, but rather the arena in which leaderships contend. The role of ordinary citizens is to provide others with power.

Just as a Marxist analysis of the Soviet Union is more deadly than any western critique, so to judge the west by the ideals of Mill's liberalism is likely to be more devastating than anything the Russians say. Each side in the 'Cold War' indicts the other for depriving the vast mass of ordinary working people of effective political power. Each frames its indictment in terms of a theory by the standards of which it too would stand indicted. Of course it remains true, as apologists for the West would argue, that there are alternative *élites* in the West, while in the Soviet Union there is only one. But this, though true, may obscure the truth that in the West rival parties within the parliamentary frame share a power of which the electorate is deprived, as effectively as it is deprived in the East, although in ways that are far more free from terror or censorship. Not that I underrate freedom from either.

The present situation in political theory presents us, therefore, both with new theoretical problems and with urgent political tasks, partly arising from questions about the role of theory itself. When we find that the two major societies in the world each tries to legitimate and justify itself by exalting a political theory the application of which would in fact show that its claims as a form of government were illegitimate and unjustified, we have to ask how in the political process itself this fact is so successfully obscured. Or is it? Does the ordinary Russian or American working-man feel deprived of power by the *élites*? If they do feel it, do they mind it? If not, how is it concealed from them? To answer these questions more fully than has yet been done would throw light on the use of theory as a weapon by government against its own citizens.

Here too the modern age is distinctive once more. The classical political theorists often offered advice to governments, usually critical advice. But apologists for government, such as Hobbes and Locke, wrote as private persons, almost as much as radical critics like Rousseau did. The theorist can now no longer be a private person. The light that he throws by theorizing must not only alter his attitudes to, but probably his treatment by, government. The apologist for contemporary oligarchy is very likely to become – if he is not already – an oligarch. To any democrat the situation outlined above obviously raises urgent practical political questions. But even to those satisfied with the *status quo* immediate practical questions arise in new theoretical forms.

For new spectres haunt the contemporary political world. One is that of the 'Third World', of the undeveloped Afro-Asian and Latin-American countries, which see themselves as deprived of power internationally by the Russo-American axis. The Third World has many distinctively different voices. But the one that is likely to be heard most insistently is that of the Chinese. And part of the Chinese polemic against not the

Russians explicitly, but the Yugoslavs (whom the Chinese habitually use as whipping-boys for the Russians) is that if you apply Marxist standards to Yugoslavia you must conclude that it is a state-capitalist power. In other words the Chinese have started to develop the theme of this talk. In so doing they are able to use Lenin himself against the Russians with great effect. When Lenin writes of the struggle between the working-class and the bourgeoisie his characteristic doctrine and his characteristic tones in *State and Revolution* are well represented by two quotations –

The petty-bourgeois democrats, those alleged Socialists who substituted dreams of class harmony for the class struggle, even pictured the Socialist reformation in a dreamy fashion – not in the form of the overthrow of the rule of the exploiting class, but in the form of the peaceful submission of the minority to the majority which has become conscious of its aims. This petty-bourgeois Utopia, which is inseparably bound up with the idea of the State being above classes, led in practice to the betrayal of the interests of the toiling classes, as was shown, for example, by the history of the French revolutions of 1848 and 1871, and by the 'Socialists' joining bourgeois cabinets in England, France, Italy and other countries at the end of the nineteenth and the beginning of the twentieth centuries.

The doctrine of the class struggle, as applied by Marx to the question of the State and of the Socialist revolution, leads inevitably to the recognition of the *political rule* of the proletariat, of its dictatorship, i.e., of power shared with none and relying directly upon the armed force of the masses. The overthrow of the bour-geoisie can be achieved only by the proletariat becoming trans-formed into the ruling class, capable of crushing the inevitable and desperate resistance of the bourgeoisie, and of organizing all the toiling and exploited masses for the new economic order.

Lenin's doctrine is: first that there can be no truce in the war between the classes; secondly that only the working class can overthrow the bourgeoisie; and thirdly that the transition from bourgeois to working-class rule cannot be peaceful. But the voice of Khrushchev and the voices of his successors, as the Chinese and Albanians have pointed out, is not the voice of Lenin. Khrushchev was in fact not unlike the dreamy socialist reformists of whom Lenin spoke. In place of violent struggle between classes he put peaceful economic competition between States; and he did not believe in the western working-class overthrowing their own bourgeoisie, but in Soviet achievements so impressing the West that in the end the western countries will make a calm and gradual transition to socialism.

The Chinese not only denounced Khrushchev for abandoning Lenin; they also thought that they knew why he was doing it. The Russians have now enriched themselves. They aspire to join the capitalist nations in peaceful harmony, just as reformist socialist leaders aspired to join bourgeois cabinets. The Russians still preserve Lenin's writings as sacred texts; but the Chinese are now able to indict the Russian ruling group of not holding the creed in which the Russian government still officially believes. We can expect much more of this. Even if the West and the Russians will not themselves face up to the discrepancy between their official theories and their actual practices, the voices of the Third World will increasingly force them to attend to it.

Obviously even so wide a range of topics as that which I have attended to in all too short a space has still left untouched vast themes. One too important not to mention finally is that of totalitarianism. It is little more than twenty years since a hitherto apparently civilized nation was marching the Jews into the gas-chambers; and even less since Stalin's monolithic police apparatus enforced its terror. It would be absurd to suppose that totalitarianism is an episode now happily and finally over, if only because we have not yet acquired the explanatory theory which would enable us to grasp why we once so nearly all fell prey to it. Any realistic political theory about our future will have to clarify for us this danger too. But the context of all such clarifications will have to be the large present conflicts which I have described. Those conflicts make it clear that theory is once again of the greatest possible practical relevance. Carlyle in a possibly apocryphal anecdote is reputed to have said to a businessman who reproached him for merely dealing in ideas: 'There was once a man called

Rousseau who wrote a book containing nothing but ideas. The second edition was bound in the skins of those who laughed at the first.' I wonder in whose skins the future editions of Marx and Mill will be bound.

BOOK-LIST

BOTTOMORE, T. B., *Elites and Society* (London, New Thinkers' Library, 1964).

DUVERGER, M., *Political Parties* (London, 1954).

LENIN, V. I., *State and Revolution* (Little Lenin Library, 1933).

OSSOWSKI, S., *Class Structure in the Social Consciousness* (London, 1963).

POPPER, K. R., *The Poverty of Historicism* (London, 1957; paperback edition 1961).

RUNCIMAN, W. G., *Social Science and Political Theory* (Cambridge, 1963).

SCHUMPETER, J. A., *Capitalism, Socialism and Democracy* (London, 1943 or later editions).

15

CONCLUSION:
THE IDEA OF EQUALITY

DAVID THOMSON

THE previous chapter touched upon theories of an *élite*, which have been one main source of doctrines of inequality in recent political thought. The other has been racialism. Doctrines of racial inequality, invoked for centuries to justify slavery, have in more recent times been used to buttress political tyranny. In this concluding chapter they may usefully be considered along with the contrasting set of ideas of social justice, security and welfare which lie behind the evolution of the 'Welfare State'. Each will be examined in relation to that central tradition of European political thought which has been the core of this symposium. Each may, in the process, cast fresh light on the nature of that tradition.

Beliefs that racial differences reflect a natural inequality among men are, no doubt, as old as European civilization. Being the most 'mongrel' of all continents Europe has never escaped awareness of the differences which exist between the races of mankind. But modern theories of racial inequality, in forms which affect political life and institutions, are mainly a product of the last hundred years. The father of them was a Frenchman, Count Arthur de Gobineau, an almost exact contemporary of Karl Marx. In 1853–5 Gobineau published a four-volume *Essay on the Inequality of Human Races*. It appeared a few years before J. S. Mill's essay *On Liberty*, Marx's *Critique of Political Economy*, and Charles Darwin's *Origin of Species*. The ideas became, therefore, part of that remarkable intellectual ferment of the 1860s and 1870s, though Gobineau seems to have been relatively little read outside Germany. There the operas of his friend, Richard Wagner, helped to disseminate similar ideas of primordial Nordic heroism and the cult of Aryan glory. A Gobineau Club was founded with Wagner as its most important member, and doctrines of racial superiority, strongly infused with anti-Semitism, became popular in artistic and intellectual circles in Germany.

The spread of such ideas was further encouraged and promoted at the end of the nineteenth century by a renegade Englishman, Houston Stewart Chamberlain (1855–1926), who became a German subject and married Wagner's daughter. His book, *The Foundations of the Nineteenth Century*, came out in 1899. It was much admired by the German Emperor, who subscribed to a fund for distributing free copies of it to all public libraries and adopted it as the bible of expansionist Pan-Germanism. Though critical of some of Gobineau's ideas, Chamberlain propagated the basic ideas of racial inequality and the need for greater racial 'purity' to ensure a strong state. What were these ideas?

Gobineau contended, in brief, that the racial divisions of mankind are inescapable and fundamental; and that obvious outward differences as regards colour of skin, type of hair, shape of nose, and so on, are accompanied by equally vivid differences of mental and emotional character. These differences are transmitted by heredity – they are a matter of bloodstock – and marriage between people of different races produces offspring with the characteristics of each in diluted form.

He argued, further, that races are not only different but unequal. Detesting the whole rationalistic and liberal tradition of the Enlightenment and the French Revolution, Gobineau held that men are born and remain *unequal*. Just as the white races are superior to the yellow, so are the yellow to the black. Yet each has its unique characteristics and merits: the black, for example, are outstandingly musical and artistic, the yellow possess the virtues that go with mediocrity and impassivity, such as law-abidingness and stability. The white (Aryan) races, however, are outstanding in vigour and inventiveness. The great civilizations have all, according to Gobineau, been founded by the initiative of the Aryans.

But, he added, some racial intermixture is advantageous. The development and progress of civilizations have often come from a moderate intermixture of races, and their culture would have been poorer without some mingling of other blood. The decline of civilizations, however, comes with excessive admixture which swamps the original stock and produces degeneration. Survival depends on a eugenic balance.

This fanciful, rather whimsical theory, decked out with a wealth of curious learning and persuasive argument, might have remained something of a cultivated Frenchman's *jeu d'esprit* had not Wagner and Chamberlain adopted it and twisted it into a much more vicious theory. Gobineau himself was not particularly pro-German: indeed, he held that the purest Aryan stock could be found among the declining French aristocracy and the British nobility. He may have derived sardonic satisfaction from the thought that Wagner's musical talents must, on his theory, have been inherited from Negro ancestry.

Chamberlain's version of the idea was that 'crossing obliterates characters', that 'the crossing of two very different types contributes to the formation of a noble race only when it takes place very seldom and is followed by strict inbreeding'. His notion of the nation-state as the protector of racial purity led straight to the 'Master Race' doctrine of Adolf Hitler and the nihilistic principles of the Third Reich –

It is almost always the nation, as a political structure, that creates the conditions for the formation of race or at least leads to the highest and most individual activities of race. Wherever, as in India, nations are not formed, the stock of strength that has been gathered by race decays ... But the firm national union is the surest protection against going astray: it signifies common memory, common hope, common intellectual nourishment; it fixes the existing bond of blood and impels us to make it ever closer.*

Hitler in *Mein Kampf* – the book, semi-autobiography and semi-treatise on racial politics, which was to become the scripture of the National-Socialist régime in Germany between

*H. S. Chamberlain, *The Foundations of the Nineteenth Century* (1911), Vol. 1, pp. 292, 294.

1933 and 1945 – quoted Chamberlain with approval. But in Hitler's handling these racial ideas became yet cruder, even more brutally inhuman. There is, Hitler believed, an 'iron law of nature' that each beast mates only with a companion of the same species. All Germany's ills sprang from inattention to the natural laws of racial inequality and purity, and especially from subservience to the Jews whom he held responsible (whether as capitalists or communists) for the degeneracy of Germany in the twentieth century. The task of the National Socialist Party, therefore, under his own inspired leadership, was to assert and ensure for a thousand years the domination of the Aryan race, the natural 'Master Race' of history. This task required a monolithic state resting on the mystical union of 'Blood and Soil' (*Blut und Erde*) and the totalitarian principles of 'One People, one State, one Leader' (*Ein Volk, ein Reich, ein Führer*). It required, therefore, bringing all German minorities within the borders of the State and, at the same time, claiming 'living-space' (*Lebensraum*) for the German people; purifying German blood by eliminating alien minorities and, above all, by exterminating the Jews; and establishing the hegemony of this State in Europe and, eventually, in the world. Hitler's 'New Order' in the parts of Europe which his armies and air-forces conquered between 1938 and 1945 was established on these principles. It left no doubt whatever about the purport of racial theories of politics. It perpetrated the greatest act of genocide in history.

Since 1945 race relations have become one of the formative forces in international relations: whether in the form of the feud between the Arab States and the new State of Israel, or the policies of *Apartheid* in South Africa and Segregation in the United States, or the relationships between Europeans and the 'Third World' of the underdeveloped countries. With the States of Africa and Asia forming a majority of members of the United Nations, racial differences in politics have assumed global importance. Can ideas of racial inequality, then, be regarded as alien and external to the central western tradition of political ideas – at most a source of protest and reaction against it? Or should they be seen, rather, as having roots within that tradition itself, a variant form of inherent impulses to exclusion, absolutism, totalitarianism which have recurred throughout the history of European civilization?

The contributions to this symposium suggest that this last possibility cannot be hastily dismissed. Machiavelli defended a form of political activity guided entirely by *raison d'état* – for statecraft geared, at all costs, to success – for a 'self-sufficient State'. Luther justified persecution of those who did not share his own religious beliefs and defended the right of a ruler to enforce religious uniformity on purely secular grounds. Hobbes formulated a 'philosophy of absolutism' which taught that 'only a unified and single power can compress an anarchy of wills into the real unity of a State'. Rousseau envisaged a State in which man could be 'forced to be free' and justified banishment of atheists as 'faithless'. Paine propounded theories of the 'Rights of Man' which were in themselves absolute dogmas, which Burke attacked with intolerant crusading fervour. Hegel was, notoriously, a state-intoxicated man who, as Professor Peters shows, 'put the stamp of philosophical respectability on doctrines which are necessary for the emergence of a totalitarian State'. Mazzini saw divisions into nations as a God-given pattern for the erection of States. It has become fashionable to argue that democratic theory itself, and even the liberal democracy of John Stuart Mill, contain an inherent propensity to illiberalism and totalitarianism.* Few would question the totalitarianism of Marxist theories, even though (as Mr MacIntyre suggests) they also contain more liberal ingredients.

In the context of these recurring tendencies racialist theories may, then, be seen as a modern counterpart or variant of those principles of exclusion, intolerance, absolutism, and claims to *élitism* which have been persistent throughout the experience of European civilization. The ecclesiastic who claims priority in salvation for his co-religionists, the nationalist who exalts his own nation's manifest destiny, the Marxist who claims moral superiority and historically inevitable victory for the

*See, for example, J. Talmon, *The Origins of Totalitarian Democracy* (1952) and M. Cowling, *Mill and Liberalism* (1963).

proletariat, are on this view not intrinsically different from the fanatical adherent of creeds of racial superiority. Both the racialist ideas themselves, and possible ways of countering them, can be better understood in the light of debate about these older political ideas.

Just as racialist ideas developed throughout the last hundred years, so likewise did ideas which culminated in the modern 'Welfare State'. They can be found, as Mr Hampden Jackson has pointed out (page 115), in the writings of Tom Paine. They owe something to the close community-consciousness and common moral purpose postulated by Rousseau's 'General Will'; to the state-paternalism of Hegel; to the deep sense of social injustice of Mill or Marx. The intellectual ingredients of each nation's conception of the Welfare State vary considerably – even as between Britain and France, though more vividly still as between the United States and the Soviet Union. Only those of Britain can be here considered.

It is possible, with enough historical ingenuity, to find rudiments of social services and public welfare in sixteenth-century Tudor paternalism, and even earlier in medieval statutes. Did not Karl de Schweinitz write of *England's Road to Social Security* 'from the Statute of Laborers in 1349 to the Beveridge Report of 1942'?* Maurice Bruce, on the other hand, seems to reserve the term 'Welfare State' for all the developments between the Elizabethan Poor Law of 1601 and the abolition of the very conception of a poor law in 1948: after which came 'the erection of a new system of social responsibility that was still not without its obligations to the aims and ideals of the Englishmen of an earlier Elizabethan age'.† It would seem preferable, as between these two extremes, to look for that growing acceptance of public responsibility, mainly exercised through the State, for protecting and promoting the 'welfare' of all citizens which can

* Published University of Pennsylvania Press, 1943; New York: Perpetua Edition, 1961.
† M. Bruce, *The Coming of the Welfare State* (London, 1961), p. 18.

be seen during the nineteenth and twentieth centuries: which leaves open the question of what is comprised within the conception of 'welfare'.

The full conception required a convergence and combination of several distinct conditions and factors: not least a national economy capable of producing enough wealth for there to be a margin for wider diffusion. The methods of production and distribution which mass-produced for mass-consumption made plenty possible. The circumstances and attitudes which created the inter-war paradox of 'poverty amid plenty' were themselves a consequence of the dislocations of the world economy and of an inadequate economic philosophy. The revolution of economic thought brought about by John Maynard Keynes (1883–1946), and by experience first of the world economic crisis (with the nightmare of mass unemployment) and then of the social security attainable even during war if appropriate methods of finance and organization were adopted, first made possible rapid development in the conception of 'Welfare' after 1945. It has become customary to regard, as the turning-point in national attitudes, the *Report on Social Insurance and Allied Services* produced in 1942 by Sir William (later Lord) Beveridge. The 'Beveridge Report' may rightly be regarded in this light, less because of its specific recommendations which were not all adopted in the form suggested, than because of the immensely important impact it had on public opinion at home and abroad.

Its three 'guiding principles' were defined by Beveridge himself –

The first principle is that any proposals for the future, while they should use to the full the experience gathered in the past, should not be restricted by consideration of sectional interests established in the obtaining of that experience ...

The second principle is that organization of social insurance should be treated as one part only of a comprehensive policy of social progress. Social insurance fully developed may provide income security; it is an attack upon Want. But Want is one only of five giants on the road of reconstruction and in some ways the easiest to attack. The others are Disease, Ignorance, Squalor and Idleness.

The third principle is that social security must be achieved by cooperation between the State and the individual. The State should offer security for service and contribution. The State in organizing security should not stifle incentive, opportunity, responsibility; in establishing a national minimum, it should leave room and encouragement for voluntary action by each individual to provide more than that minimum for himself and his family.*

If these principles were quickly accepted by all political parties in Britain – and if they struck responsive chords in the Commonwealth, the United States, and many European countries – this was largely because the time was ripe for the exploration and implementation of a new outlook in social policy. Tentative and piecemeal measures, adopted partially and applied in a fragmentary way, no longer had an appeal. The war-time and post-war mood favoured more comprehensive plans, as well as more energetic efforts, to attain the full employment of resources and planned economic growth, the systematic improvement of social conditions, and what President Franklin D. Roosevelt described as 'freedom from want' and 'freedom from fear'.

But no more than the mood which proved so receptive to them did Beveridge's principles spring unheralded from the situation in Britain in 1942. Behind his thinking – as behind much of the thinking of Maynard Keynes – lay a fruitful combination of experience and of political ideas: experience of what had been and what might be achieved by more active and concerted public concern with problems of want, and a set of political ideas which, since the 1880s, had nourished many liberal and socialist thinkers. The ideas were mostly associated with the liberal-idealist philosophy of Thomas Hill Green (1836–82), whose influence upon a whole generation and more of Oxford scholars was truly remarkable. Green, an Oxford don, was a Gladstonian liberal in politics and a protagonist of humanist and Christian values against the influence of both utilitarian and Darwinian ideas,

*Cmd. 6404 (1942), pp. 6–7.

which he regarded as equally debasing. In the quarter-century before 1914, during which much social legislation was passed by the Liberal governments, Green's ideas permeated social thought in England. They influenced the new Master of Balliol, Edward Caird, and an army of Balliol men which included Asquith, Bernard Bosanquet, William Beveridge, R. H. Tawney, William Temple, A. D. Lindsay and Ernest Barker. They infiltrated the Fabian Society and so came to exert some influence on the newly formed Labour Party. They spread wide and sank deep because they were in the direct English evangelical tradition of philanthropic humanitarianism.*

What, then, were the central ideas of Green's philosophy? Nurtured on one hand in the traditions of Greek philosophy and of German idealist philosophy (especially Kant and Hegel), on the other in the powerful traditions of English Nonconformity and piety, Green's political thought was an unstable equilibrium between the appeals of the community and of the individual. Individual freedom and fulfilment, he insisted, are attainable only through society. He believed fervently that 'there is a work of moral liberation which society, through its various agencies, is constantly carrying on for the individual'. And by 'society' he meant not only the State –

The other forms of community which precede and are independent of the formation of the State, do not continue to exist outside it, nor yet are they superseded by it. They are carried on into it. They become its organic members, supporting its life and in turn maintained by it in a new harmony with each other.†

The State, in short, is a community of communities, and one of its chief functions is to serve as an adjustment-centre for the claims of individuals and societies upon one another. By means of this intensely pluralistic conception of the State Green tempered the totalitarian tendencies of idealist thought and kept room in his philosophy for the rich diversity of

* *See* M. Richter, *The Politics of Conscience: T. H. Green and his Age* (London, 1964), Chapter 10.

† T. H. Green, *Lectures on the Principles of Political Obligation* (London, 1931 edition), p. 146. The Lectures were first delivered in 1879–80.

opinions and interests, groups and associations, which constitute an 'open society'.

After Green the concept of the 'common good' which men pursue within society through the agency of the State could less readily be discussed in utilitarian terms of material interests alone: the notion of 'welfare' now implied not only 'social welfare' but also 'moral welfare'. Beveridge's five giants clearly cannot be vanquished by economic progress alone, although a rise in the standard of living is a prerequisite of success against them. Victory against all five presupposes a State with an overriding concern for welfare, devoting not merely marginal activities but its basic energies to such provision. Only when the purpose of social security and welfare becomes dominant does it become strictly accurate to speak of 'the Welfare State'. Now that even the external activities of the modern State are almost as much concerned with cooperation for human welfare as with preparation for national defence, the label becomes very apt.* Just as the racial theory of the State is the climax of a century or more of developing ideas of racial inequality, so the idea of the Welfare State is the apotheosis of a couple of centuries of political activity guided by the ideal of human equality and social justice.

World politics are now, to a great extent, the result of a clash between conditions of inequality and ideals of equality. As political independence and equality of status have been won by peoples of Asia and Africa formerly subject to European rule, dramatic inequalities of standard of living have become more important. Retarded in their economic progress by the 'population explosion' happening whilst their natural resources were still underdeveloped, the peoples of the 'Third World' remain dependent upon financial and technical aid from the more technologically advanced countries. The fact that they are 'coloured' peoples makes for racial inequalities on a global scale.

It may come to seem, in the future, that current conflicts of

*Compare R. M. Titmuss, *Essays on 'The Welfare State'* (London, 1958), especially Chapter 2, and G. Myrdal, *Beyond the Welfare State* (London, 1960), especially Chapters 5 and 14.

political ideas are concerned less with issues of dictatorship versus democracy, the claims of the community as against the rights of the individual, and the complex of issues usually associated with the ideal of Liberty: and that they are even more directly concerned with the ideal of Equality. If so, it may then become apparent that the debate about political ideas which has been traced in these pages is a continuing debate. The idea that, despite the curse of Cain, men should learn to live like brothers remains one of the most persistent of all political and social ideas in our civilization.

BOOK-LIST

A good understanding of racialist ideas can be gained from reading ALAN BULLOCK's biography of Hitler: *A Study in Tyranny* (London, 1952; Penguin Books edition, 1960), and of the idea of the Welfare State from the books already quoted. The following general studies may also be of interest –

MILLER, J. D. B., *The Nature of Politics* (London, 1962, Pelican Book 1965).

MOSSE, G. L., *The Culture of Western Europe: The Nineteenth and Twentieth Centuries* (New York, 1961, London 1963).

TAWNEY, R. H., *Equality* (London, 1931; rev. ed. with a new introduction by R. M. Titmuss, 1964).

THOMSON, D., *Equality* (Cambridge, 1949); and *England in the Twentieth Century* (London, 1964; Pelican Books 1965).

INDEX

Absolutism, 17, 54, 55, 84, 96, 137–40, 195

Africa, 12, 93, 138, 174, 187, 194, 200

America (U.S.A.), 13–14, 19–20, 55, 77, 90, 93, 107–8, 110, 116, 138, 155, 169, 173, 183, 186–7, 194, 196, 198

Aristocracy, 82, 84, 86–7, 89, 109, 127. See also Whigs

Aristotle (384–322 B.C.), 12, 59, 73, 86

Armed forces of State, 26–7, 91, 134, 152

Augustine, St (353–430), 12, 42, 43, 58

Bentham, Jeremy (1748–1832), 15, 116, 157

Beveridge, William Henry, 1st Baron (1879–1963), 103, 196–200

Bismarck, Prince Otto von (1815–98), 33, 135

Borgia, Cesare (1476–1507), 23, 25, 28

Bosanquet, Bernard (1848–1923), 134, 199

Bradley, Francis Herbert (1846–1924), 134

Burke, Edmund (1729–97), Chap. 9 passim and 13, 14, 16, 18, 81, 108, 131, 169, 195

Calvin, John (1509–64), 15, 35, 51, 104

Capitalism, Chap. 13 passim and 15, 66, 145–6, 148, 184, 194

Chamberlain, Houston Stewart (1855–1927), 192–4

Charles I, King of England (1600–1649), 54

Charles II, King of England (1630–85), 70–73, 74–5

Checks and balances of power, 13, 61, 64, 89–90

China, 12, 14, 83, 187–9

Christendom, 17, 25, 31, 33, 83

Churches, 12, 22, 35–6, 39, 100–101, 113

Church–State, 15, 35–6, 39–51

City-State, 23, 98, 130, 138

Classes in society, 16, 140–41, 155, 169–74, 183–9

'Cold War', 14, 181, 186

Communism, Chapter 13 passim and 14, 15, 148, 181–5, 194

Community, as an organism, 16, 96–8, 123–4, 128, 130, 199–200

Consent, to government, 12, 64, 75–7, 96

Conservatism, 14, 77, 126–9

Constitutional government, 89, 111–12, 130, 115–16, 121, 123–4, 127. See also Representative government, Republican government

Darwin, Charles Robert (1809–82), 161, 191

Declaration of American Independence (1776), 13, 19–20, 112

Declaration of the Rights of Man (1789), 19, 112–15, 119

Democracy, 86–7, 99–104, 108, 114–15, 120, 127, 148–9, 153, 155, 166, 181–2, 186–8. See also Constitutional government, Representative government

Dialectic, 131, 135–6, 140–41

Divine Right of Kings, 51, 75, 77, 96

Economics and politics, 16, 104–5, 114–15, 151, 168–79, 197–8, 200
Education, 62–3, 86, 95, 107, 115, 134, 147–8, 150, 157
Élites, nature and role of in society, 16, 56–7, 185–9, 191, 195–6
Empire, Holy Roman, 12, 22, 48
Engels, Friedrich (1820–95), 16, 168
England, 12, 13, 18, 51, 54, 63, 70–77, 89, 97, 107–8, 116, 127, 134, 155–7, 168, 180, 196
Equality, Chap. 15 *passim* and 57, 77, 100, 105, 112, 114, 148, 151–2
Europe, 11, 14, 17, 20, 146, 147, 150, 168, 176, 191, 194. *See also under separate countries*
Existentialism, 139

Fascism, 15, 135, 141. *See also* Hitler, Adolf
Florence, 23, 25–6, 30, 32, 176
France, 12, 13, 18, 23, 27, 71, 77, 87, 108, 110–13, 116, 150, 192, 193, 196
Freedom, 15, 16, 18, 60, 70, 76, 78–80, 85, 92, 104, 112–14, 125, 132–3, 135–6, 148, 150, 154ff., 199–201

Gandhi, Mohandas Karamchand (1869–1948), 143–5, 149
'General Will', 97–100, 102, 150, 196
Germany, 13, 23, 35, 37, 45, 89, 130–31, 134–5, 138, 168, 186, 191–4, 199
Gobineau, Joseph Arthur, Count de (1816–82), 191–3
Greeks, ancient, 12, 17, 88, 110, 130, 135–6, 138, 199. *See also* Aristotle, Plato, Rome
Green, Thomas Hill (1836–82), 15, 198–200

Hegel, Georg Wilhelm Friedrich (1770–1831), Chap. 10 *passim* and 13, 33, 51, 147, 169, 195, 196, 199
History and politics, 14, 24–5, 42, 124, 130, 132, 134, 135, 138–9, 148–9, 170, 193–5
Hitler, Adolf (1889–1945), 15, 17, 33, 34, 97, 147, 193–4
Hobbes, Thomas (1588–1679), Chap. 4 *passim* and 12, 14–15, 17, 34, 43, 82, 96, 187, 195
Hume, David (1711–76), 63, 131

Ideologies in politics, 13–14, 15, 77, 90, 128–9
Imperialism, 20, 77, 134
India, 12, 88, 143–4, 149–50
Individuality, ideas of, 14, 16–18, 65–6, 123, 132–3, 147–8, 163–4, 197–201
Industrialization, 13–14, 67, 102, 169–77. *See also* Economics and politics
Interests, theories of, 12, 16, 20, 28, 85, 97–8, 99, 132–3, 146, 164–5, 170, 197
Internationalism, 20, 131, 149, 151–2, 194
Italy, 13, 23–6, 134, 143–7, 148, 150–51

James II, King of England (1633–1701), 73, 75–6
Jefferson, Thomas (1743–1826), 18, 116
Justice:
under law, 65, 111, 125, 133, 136
social, 103, 125, 196–200

Kant, Immanuel (1724–1804), 130–31, 199

Keynes, John Maynard, 1st Baron (1883–1946), 171, 197–8

Knowledge, theories of, 67–8, 79, 84

Law, 13, 16, 76, 87, 110, 113

Lenin, Vladimir Ilyich (1870–1924), 19, 145, 179, 185–6, 188–9

Liberalism, traditions of, 13–14, 129, 132, 185, 191, 198–200

Liberty: see Freedom

Locke, John (1632–1704), Chap. 5 passim and 12–15, 16, 19, 57, 89, 96, 101, 107, 131, 133, 187

Louis XII, King of France (1462–1515), 23, 27

Louis XIV, King of France (1638–1715), 71

Luther, Martin (1483–1546), Chap. 3 passim and 12, 16, 101, 130, 195

Machiavelli, Niccolo di Bernardo dei (1469–1527), Chap. 2 passim and 12, 16–18, 34, 58, 87, 96, 176, 195

Marx, Karl (1818–83), Chap. 13 passim and 14, 17, 19, 66, 82, 128, 140–41, 145, 181–91, 195–6

Mazzini, Giuseppe (1805–72), Chap. 11 passim and 13–15, 195

Mechanistic ideas in politics, 16, 54–5, 123–4

Melanchthon, Philip (1497–1560), 47

Mill, John Stuart (1806–73), Chap. 12 passim and 14–16, 75, 169, 181, 183, 190, 191, 195, 196

Monarchy, 70, 86, 88, 109, 115, 119, 134, 150. See also Divine Right of Kings

Montesquieu, Charles de Secondat, Baron de la Brède et de (1689–1755), Chap. 6 passim and 12, 18–19, 96

Morals and politics, 22, 28–33, 84–5, 87, 100, 102–3, 121–2, 128, 133, 156, 164–5

Nationality, principle of, 13, 104, 109, 113, 137, 145–53, 195

Nation-State, 13, 98, 102, 111, 138–9, 146–50, 151–2, 193

'Nature':
idea of, 68, 84, 92, 95, 102, 136–7
rights of, 77–8, 96, 111–12, 121
state of, 55–6, 59–60, 75, 137

Non-resistance, doctrine of, 36–7, 43–5

Obedience, 16, 35, 40, 44–5, 60, 75, 109

Opinion, 12, 16, 148, 156–7, 160–63

Paine, Thomas (1737–1809), Chap. 8 passim and 12, 14, 17, 18, 19, 57, 120, 196

Parties in politics, 97–100, 127, 182–6

Passions in politics, 54–5, 118, 121–2, 128

Plato (c. 427–c. 347 B.C.), 12, 75, 135

Pluralist ideas, 20, 100, 133, 199–200

'Power politics', 18, 29–30, 41, 59–60, 65, 90, 151–2

Property, 57, 62, 78, 104–5, 112–13

Punishment, 41, 62, 90

Racial ideas, 17, 148–9, 189, 191–6, 200–201

Radicalism, 13, 15, 107–16, 120, 129, 147

Reason, 15, 17, 55, 63, 67–8, 77, 84, 119–23, 131, 136–7, 144, 192

Reformation, 22, 37, 38, 47

Religion and politics, 22, 33, 34–52, 54, 63–4, 68–9, 72–3, 86, 92, 100–101, 119–20, 130, 131–2, 137–9, 149, 168–9, 195

Renaissance, 12, 31, 37

Representative government, 13, 98, 110–11, 114, 185–6. *See also* Constitutional government, Republican government

Republican government, 30–32, 86–9, 110, 146. *See also* Constitutional government, Representative government

Revolution:
theories of, 44–6, 51, 59, 71, 76–9, 112, 116, 118–25, 128–9, 145, 152, 179, 184–5, 188–9
English (1688–9), 71–7, 89, 115, 120–21
French (1789), 13, 14, 19, 77, 100, 104, 105, 108, 118–21, 130–31, 145, 152, 182, 192
Russian (1917), 14, 77, 152, 183–5

Rights, theories of, 13, 62, 64–5, 77–8, 96, 108, 111–12, 121, 145–6

Rome, ancient, 17, 23, 24, 71, 88–9, 136

Rousseau, Jean-Jacques (1712–78), Chap. 7 *passim* and 12–14, 17–19, 34, 57, 82, 92, 118, 130, 131, 138, 169, 182, 187, 190, 195–6

Russia (U.S.S.R.), 14, 77, 152, 181–4, 196

Science, 17, 55, 60, 67, 70–71, 75, 83, 86, 109–10, 136, 165, 181–2

Shaftesbury, Anthony Ashley Cooper, 1st Earl of (1621–83), 71–3, 74, 76

'Social Contract' theories, 14, 55, 75–7, 95–9, 111, 126

Socialism, 15, 103–4, 129, 146, 188

Sovereignty, 12–14, 60–64, 75, 97–8, 101, 103, 105, 109, 113, 151–2

Spain, 12, 28, 53

Stalin, Joseph (1879–1953), 15, 181, 184, 189

Tawney, Richard Henry (1880–1962), 34, 199

Tocqueville, Alexis de (1805–59), 16, 155

Toleration, 49, 72, 101, 131

Totalitarianism, 15, 100, 133, 181–5, 189, 194–5, 199

Trade Unions, 97, 99–100, 127, 177

United Nations, 152, 194

Utilitarianism, 15, 112, 128, 157–9, 165, 198. *See also* Bentham, J., Mill, J. S.

Voltaire, François Marie Arouet de (1694–1778), 63, 83, 92, 101, 130

Wagner, Richard (1813–83), 192–3

'Welfare State', 90–91, 103, 191, 196–201

Whigs, 14, 71, 89

William III, King of England (1650–1702), 73–4, 77

Wilson, President Thomas Woodrow (1856–1924), 13, 147

FOR THE BEST IN PAPERBACKS, LOOK FOR THE

In every corner of the world, on every subject under the sun, Penguin represents quality and variety – the very best in publishing today.

For complete information about books available from Penguin – including Pelicans, Puffins, Peregrines and Penguin Classics – and how to order them, write to us at the appropriate address below. Please note that for copyright reasons the selection of books varies from country to country.

In the United Kingdom: For a complete list of books available from Penguin in the U.K., please write to *Dept E.P., Penguin Books Ltd, Harmondsworth, Middlesex, UB7 0DA*

In the United States: For a complete list of books available from Penguin in the U.S., please write to *Dept BA, Penguin, 299 Murray Hill Parkway, East Rutherford, New Jersey 07073*

In Canada: For a complete list of books available from Penguin in Canada, please write to *Penguin Books Canada Ltd, 2801 John Street, Markham, Ontario L3R 1B4*

In Australia: For a complete list of books available from Penguin in Australia, please write to the *Marketing Department, Penguin Books Australia Ltd, P.O. Box 257, Ringwood, Victoria 3134*

In New Zealand: For a complete list of books available from Penguin in New Zealand, please write to the *Marketing Department, Penguin Books (NZ) Ltd, Private Bag, Takapuna, Auckland 9*

In India: For a complete list of books available from Penguin, please write to *Penguin Overseas Ltd, 706 Eros Apartments, 56 Nehru Place, New Delhi, 110019*

In Holland: For a complete list of books available from Penguin in Holland, please write to *Penguin Books Nederland B.V., Postbus 195, NL–1380AD Weesp, Netherlands*

In Germany: For a complete list of books available from Penguin, please write to *Penguin Books Ltd, Friedrichstrasse 10 – 12, D–6000 Frankfurt Main 1, Federal Republic of Germany*

In Spain: For a complete list of books available from Penguin in Spain, please write to *Longman Penguin España, Calle San Nicolas 15, E–28013 Madrid, Spain*

A CHOICE OF PENGUINS AND PELICANS

The Second World War (6 volumes)   Winston S. Churchill

The definitive history of the cataclysm which swept the world for the second time in thirty years.

1917: The Russian Revolutions and the Origins of Present-Day Communism
Leonard Schapiro

A superb narrative history of one of the greatest episodes in modern history by one of our greatest historians.

Imperial Spain 1496–1716   J. H. Elliot

A brilliant modern study of the sudden rise of a barren and isolated country to be the greatest power on earth, and of its equally sudden decline. 'Outstandingly good' – *Daily Telegraph*

Joan of Arc: The Image of Female Heroism   Marina Warner

'A profound book, about human history in general and the place of women in it' – Christopher Hill

Man and the Natural World: Changing Attitudes in England 1500–1800
Keith Thomas

'A delight to read and a pleasure to own' – Auberon Waugh in the *Sunday Telegraph*

The Making of the English Working Class   E. P. Thompson

Probably the most imaginative – and the most famous – post-war work of English social history.